# TALK

# IS

# CHEAP

## THE FIGHT AGAINST MEDIOCRITY

# TALK

# IS

# CHEAP

## THE FIGHT AGAINST MEDIOCRITY

**The only way to separate yourself from the pack and achieve your true potential.**

Kevin Kartchner

IV

Talk Is Cheap - The Fight Against Mediocrity

By Kevin Kartchner

Publisher: POFG, LLC

Paperback - ISBN: 979-8-9851680-3-7

Cover design by Kevin Kartchner

Printed in the United States of America

# ACKNOWLEDGEMENTS

To my wonderful wife, Lauren. She is constantly pushing me to achieve my goals. Someone told me that the longer they've been married the more they love their spouse. I second that. I love this crazy journey called life that we get to conquer together. I love you, Lauren.

As cliché as it sounds, I could fill this entire book with the names of those who have blessed my life. You know who you are. Thank you.

To you, the reader, for not only supporting me, but also aspiring to be better.

# CONTENTS

# FOREWORD

To be honest, I hate reading the foreword and usually skip it. Let's get straight to the meat and potatoes.

The way to get started is to quit talking and begin doing.

WALT DISNEY

x

# INTRODUCTION

## DELUSION

**"When you are mediocre you are the best of the worst and the worst of the best." —David L. Beck**

Do you have goals or dreams that have been sitting on the back burner? Have you written the same New Year's resolutions year after year and abandoned them after just a few weeks? Are you sick and tired of being sick and tired? Do you feel that mediocrity is a sin against your potential and that you have greatness inside of you? If you answered yes to any of these questions, then this book was written for you.

My purpose is to help you reach the next level of success (and then the next and the next) and accomplish the goals you've always dreamed of achieving. I want to inspire you to *act* on your deepest goals, dreams, and desires (because *Talk Is*

*Cheap*) while showing you what it truly takes to separate yourself from the pack or society surrounding you (*Fight Mediocrity*).

Who am I? My name is Kevin Kartchner. I am not Superman, and I am definitely not perfect. I like to be lazy, lie around on the couch, and often put off things I know I should be doing. I am also no more capable than you. I just happen to have lived through a unique series of events that taught me the secret to great success.

I spent two years living in the beautiful Riviera Maya of Mexico serving as a full-time missionary for the Church of Jesus Christ of Latter-Day Saints. (Don't worry, you don't have to be religious to read this book.) I had volunteered to serve for two years as a missionary to invite others to come unto Jesus Christ. I served with no pay, in a country I'd never lived in, speaking a language I did not know, and to top it off, I was paired with a companion (we taught in pairs) who didn't speak a word of English. It was one of the most challenging experiences of my life.

I wish I could say my mission was a big success from the start, but it wasn't. We set big goals as a companionship to help a certain number of people come unto Christ and be baptized, planned, and did absolutely nothing. We essentially taught the same six people every week for three months. These six people would listen to us, but they didn't really want to take action. It was a long three months. We didn't hit any of our goals, and it was extremely discouraging. I was there to help people, and it didn't seem like we were helping anyone.

Then, after three months, I received a new companion who was on the last six weeks of his two-year mission. His name is Chente, he was from Mexico, and he was about half my height. (I'm six-foot four for reference.) Chente told me that he could hardly read when he first arrived on his mission. He made significant sacrifices to serve. He was also one of the hardest workers I've ever met. As soon as we teamed up, he took me aside and told me that we were going to achieve massive goals over the next six weeks. I believed we could, (I was all about the big goals) but I'd never achieved any of my goals thus far in my mission. I was terrified what he might think or say when he found out how little I had actually done.

As he opened our area book for the first time, I felt like I was going to pass out. Chente was about to see all the work I had done…which wasn't much. What would he say? I felt so embarrassed that I taught the same people for nearly three months. Would he tell the other missionaries how lazy I was? It wasn't like I felt good about it! I started to think about all the rebuttals I would use to combat his accusations. I felt ashamed and started praying that the house would crumble on top of me so I could hide from the truth.

Chente started flipping through the pages of the area book like a detective reviews a crime scene. Every page revealed the truth of the last three months; there was no more hiding. I waited for him to look at me with disgust and disappointment. There was a small fan blowing in my direction, but I still felt like I was in the middle of a volcano. He had figured me out: he knew I was all talk. As he turned the last page, he slowly looked up at me. He said absolutely nothing. He just looked at me, and I knew things were going to change. He looked at me with conviction, with resolve. He looked at me as if to say, "We're gonna turn this ship around." That's when Chente taught me the missing piece to my success and how to truly separate myself from the pack. I made the decision right then and there that I would do whatever Chente taught me.

Now, before I tell you what he taught me, let me tell you why I achieved so little before he arrived. I grew up thinking all you had to do was visualize your goals. I learned this in a documentary named *The Secret*. If you've read the book or watched the movie, then you know it's all about visualization and the law of attraction. The movie shared story after story of individuals who visualized their desired outcomes and miraculously, through the law of attraction, attained it and transformed their lives. I was sold. I started visualizing everything, and like a customer at a restaurant, I waited for the chef to complete my order. It seemed so easy, almost too easy, maybe even suspiciously easy . . .

I loved writing down goals. I had goals for money, possessions, grades in school, relationships, etc. I'd have a goal, write it down—and then do nothing. A great formula for success, I know. I was big on motivation, I wanted it, but just in my head. My hands and feet, my actions, didn't reflect my inner desires. One of my goals was to buy this $2,000 shiny red go-cart! I'd spend hours researching the go-cart, everything from its top speed to the tire tread and everything in between. I imagined riding around the block and impressing all my friends in my shiny red go-cart. I imagined the wind flowing through my flattop. (Hey, my grandpa gave me my haircuts; give me a break.) I wrote down the goal in the present tense, visualized, and waited anxiously for my go-cart! A week passed by, then two weeks, then two months, and nothing changed. It didn't show up at my front door like the movie said it would. I started getting frustrated. It was supposed to just appear! What was I doing wrong? It felt like my dreams were so far out of reach. Was I unworthy of the go-cart? I felt like I was doomed to a life of never achieving my goals. This frustration followed me during my teenage years and into my mission.

So, when Chente came along, he added the missing element to my visualizing: ACTION. The next six weeks changed my life, and I don't say that lightly. Chente was the coach I needed to take me to the next level. Everything we were taught to do as missionaries, he executed, then went above and beyond with extreme discipline and speed. He was committed to achieving the goals: they weren't just pretty words on a piece of paper; they were targets to be annihilated. We talked to every person at every moment of every day. We talked to people and invited them to learn about Jesus Christ on our morning run, in the taxi, at the grocery store, in the streets, at the barbershop, everywhere we went. We invited every person to meet with us and make commitments to learn more. We were rejected thousands of times! We were accepted a large portion of the time as well! We would have so many appointments that we had to request permission to split up and have other church members come with us to complete them all. It was a complete 180-degree turn from the previous three months. Chente and I started to see enormous results. The results continued to grow during our time together. It was the first time in my life I felt like I had a direct impact on the completion of a goal instead of just wishing for results.

One night as I was lying in my hammock (it was extremely hot and humid, so we slept in hammocks), it dawned on me why the go-cart never appeared on my doorstep. What *The Secret* had taught me about visualization was important, **but without action, I was living in a state of**

**delusion**. I had the equation backward. I was trying to change the laws of achievement. Effort doesn't lie: talk lies. If, instead of dreaming about the go-cart, I would have gotten off the couch and worked from dawn to dusk, then the go-cart would have been mine. But I didn't. I sat there and talked about how cool it would have been but didn't **DO** anything about it. It was as if I'd discovered the missing puzzle piece to achievement that had been hidden for my entire life. I finally felt like I controlled my destiny. I wasn't at the mercy of some mystery chef who may or may not deliver my "go-cart goals" to my front door.

A few days later, we were eating lunch with some of the church members in the area. It was an extremely hot day, and we had a full calendar of appointments. As we ate, I felt overjoyed about all the progress we had made. It didn't feel real. We had witnessed so many amazing things happen, and it was the happiest I'd been since arriving to Mexico. Then reality sunk it when someone asked, "Chente, when do you go home?" It felt like everyone around me started talking and moving in slow motion. I felt a knot build up in my stomach, and it wasn't from the food. He was leaving in just one week. I started having flashbacks of the days before Chente had arrived and changed my life. Maybe I could convince him to stay? Not likely: he hadn't seen his family in two years. Was I doomed to repeat my past failures? For the remainder of the day, I couldn't stop thinking about what would happen after Chente went home.

For the next week, I couldn't stop dreading the day I would have to drop Chente off at the mission offices. I felt like he was my Mr. Miyagi and I still needed so much training if I was ever going to defeat Cobra Kai. That's the thing about time: it doesn't stop for anyone. Chente did go home, and I received a new companion. As my new companion and I sat on the bus back to our area, I realized that I couldn't go back to the way things were. I couldn't let Chente down, I couldn't let God down, and I couldn't let the people I was teaching down. I felt it my moral obligation to not only continue practicing what Chente taught me during my mission, but for the rest of my life. If I could sum up my time with Chente in just three words they would be: *Talk Is Cheap*!

Chente taught me that I needed to learn from people who were doing more than I was, so upon returning from my mission, I started diving into more and more self-development material. If *The Secret* had failed to mention the crucial step of taking action, then what else was I missing? What was holding me back? I started listening to motivational YouTube videos while I was at work for nearly eight hours per day. In fact, I can recite some of Arnold Schwarzenegger's speeches word for word. As I started consuming more and more content, I began to learn ideas that weren't taught to me in college and that almost no one around me was talking about, let alone implementing. I started writing down all these teachings in journals and on sticky notes. I taped the sticky notes to the back of my phone so I constantly had a reference. I was determined to internalize the mindset of the top 1% so I could separate myself from the pack.

This book is a summary of the discoveries I've made on my self-development journey. I've spent thousands of hours compiling this information, testing it, and weeding out the crap and the gimmicks. I don't want you to suffer like I did, trying to find these principles that aren't taught in college and no one seems to talk about. I want to give you the "fast pass" so you don't have to go through what I did.

By following the simple principles outlined in this book, anyone can achieve their goals and dreams of becoming excellent. Anyone can incorporate these principles into their life. I'm the guinea pig: I've tried and tested what I'm about to share with you and I've seen tremendous results. I would like to mention that, without the help of amazing people in my life, these accomplishments would not be possible. When I hear other success stories, it inspires me and helps me believe that I can succeed just like them. As I'll expand on in Chapter 8, there is no such thing as a self-made man or woman. We all receive help along the way. The only reason I share any of this with you is because I want you to know that I'm not special, and if I can do it, then you can do it too. I feel like I'm just getting started. Here are just a few things I have done with the knowledge I'll share in this book:

- Increased my income by five times over the last three years;
- Accumulated a net worth of $1 million at age 27;
- Gained nearly forty pounds of muscle (so I am no longer confused with a string bean);
- Completed triathlons and did the biking portion on a unicycle (yeah, those things with just one wheel!);
- Ranked 2nd in North America in street unicycling and 4th in the world;
- Became the top sales agent and later promoted to director of sales at two different companies;
- Spent over $70,000 in the last two years on coaching and self-development;
- Bought my wife a Tesla Model X (her dream car!);
- Graduated in 1.5 years with a Master's degree in Real Estate Development.

So, let me ask you: what do you want to put on your list of accomplishments? If you could do anything you wanted, what would you do? Don't worry about the past. Don't worry about the future. Just worry about the now. Now is the time to get to work! Now is the time to take action. It doesn't need to be perfect: JUST START.

> PRO TIP: As you read, you will receive inspiration (oftentimes not from the words I write, but from the thoughts you receive) for your life. Write it down so you don't forget the inspiration you receive and take action!

# CHAPTER 0

---

# WHAT IS MEDIOCRITY?

**"Mediocrity is not valued." —Kevin Kartchner**

Why chapter 0? Because in order for any of this to make sense, you need to know what mediocrity is and why I'm fighting it. We need to start at the beginning.

I always sensed the need to fight mediocrity, but I was never able to describe the feeling with words. Then, one day while I was at the gym listening to one of Darren Hardy's books, he expressed that sometimes hatred can be a more powerful motivator for someone than love, that sometimes people find their passion not based on what they love but on what they hate. He explained that, if you love something, there is automatically an adversary attached to it. For example, there is God, but there is also Satan. We have the sun, but we also have the moon. You get the point. "Well, I love success and achieving big goals," I thought to myself. That's when it hit me like a ton of bricks and **THE FIGHT AGAINST MEDIOCRITY** was born. When I said it out loud, I got the chills. It was as if someone grabbed a cup of gas and threw it on the flames of passion inside me. It felt like putting the last jagged piece into a puzzle I'd been working on my entire life. It felt like home, and I knew there was no going back.

From that moment on, I felt obligated to spread the movement with anyone who would listen. I felt I was being guided to share what I was feeling. Every morning at the gym, I'd have to pause multiple times to write down what I can only describe as inspiration for what would be in this book. I knew I needed to share what I was learning about mediocrity with the world.

---

PRO TIP: When I say *success* or *successful*, I'm not saying everyone must be defined by the world's definition of success. Success is different for everyone. *Successful* as defined by Merriam-Webster Dictionary is "the satisfactory accomplishment of a goal sought for."

---

The word *mediocre* comes from the Latin word *mediocris*, meaning "medium size, moderate, middling, commonplace, and halfway to the top" (Merriam-Webster). What does "halfway to the top" mean? Is being mediocre when someone only reaches half of their full potential?

A tree that is capable of growing one hundred feet high doesn't reach fifty feet and say, "Well, the view is okay from here. I'm going to stop growing now." NO! I firmly believe that the greatest thief of success is mediocrity.

We were made in the image of God, and each of us has divine potential. One day we will see what we could have been if we would have fought mediocrity. It is your moral obligation to do whatever you can to become the best version of yourself. The alternative is mediocrity. There is pain on both sides of the coin. There will be pain as you fight mediocrity, but the alternative is the pain of knowing you were capable of more. The pain of knowing you could have done more will haunt you forever.

If I haven't made myself clear up to this point, I am fighting mediocrity. I'm out for blood. I hate, disdain, and abhor mediocrity. It is something I do not tolerate. Mediocrity is my Darth Vader. I'm sorry if I led you to believe it was just a catchy slogan, but The Fight Against Mediocrity is my battle cry and a worldwide movement.

*Fight* is defined as the following in Merriam-Webster:

**Fight - verb**

**fought**\ 'fȯt \; **fighting**

*intransitive verb*

**1**: to contend in battle or physical combat

*especially*: to strive to overcome a person by blows or weapons

The soldiers *fought* bravely.

**2**: to put forth a determined effort

They were *fighting* to stay awake.

**3**: to contend against in or as if in battle or physical combat

They *fought* the invaders of his homeland.

**4**: to attempt to prevent the success or effectiveness of

The company *fought* the takeover attempt.

Now let me tell you, there is a big difference between *playing* with improvement and *fighting* for improvement. You must *fight* for it. If you knew someone was going to harm your friends and family, you would fight back. You love them, and you'd do whatever it took. Some of the most world-changing moments have occurred because someone was willing to fight for what they believed in. Despite being outnumbered, they gave their lives for what they believed in. You, too, must make the decision that enough is enough and choose to fight! You are outnumbered, but what the enemy doesn't have is your will to win. You're fighting for your family, your future, and your potential. I will provide you with the weapons, but you must develop the feeling and attitude of enlisting in the army and fighting mediocrity.

I'm waging a revolutionary war on mediocrity. It has ruled for far too long and must be dethroned. Its grip is white-knuckled on the dreams of far too many. Like a thief in the night, it has robbed them of their ambitions and potential. Mediocrity lurks and attacks when you least expect it. No one is immune from its effects. If you aren't careful, you, too, will fall victim to its chains of death.

Society would have you believe that the outcome of this war has already been decided; It wants you to just sit back and "be grateful for what you have." I know you feel differently. I know you desire to go against society and prove everyone wrong. You've always had big goals and dreams but felt like you were looked down upon for voicing them. I'm giving you permission to fight.

It's time to stand up and take a definitive stance. The armor and weapons of war provided in this book will guarantee your success, but only if you make the commitment to never again turn back. Let me make this clear: mediocrity is strategizing right now, this very moment, to destroy your future potential. It is enraged every time you pursue excellence and greatness. It will stop at nothing to take total control of your life. Your choice is not to wage war; the war has already begun. Your choice is whether to pick up your weapons of war and FIGHT.

So, what do you say? Are you willing to join The Fight Against Mediocrity? Write down below what you will do today to join The Fight Against Mediocrity.

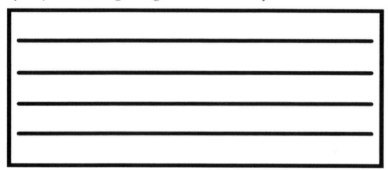

I didn't accomplish my goal of buying a go-cart because THERE WAS NO ACTION. I was under the false impression that, if I just wrote down my goals and thought about it all the time, then somehow my go-cart would just appear in the driveway. I was experiencing what Jim Rohn explained when he said, "Inspiration without action leads to delusion." I was delusional. I was missing a big part of the formula of achievement: ACTION.

This book will not only teach you the principles needed to succeed, but also how to apply them to your life. The foundation upon which The Fight Against Mediocrity is built is ACTION. Without action, everything comes tumbling down.

Disraeli said it best: "Life is too short to be little." It's too short to play small. It's definitely too short to waste years settling for below your potential. No one is truly okay with mediocrity. We are all like a big redwood tree. The redwood tree that has the ability to grow to 250 feet is going to grow the full 250 feet. It will grow to its maximum potential. Its **natural inclination** is to do so. Humans have the same innate desire, but throughout our lives we are rejected, shut down, and told no. Frankly, we are surrounded by mediocrity everywhere we turn. Here are some very startling stats about average America:

- According to Staff Squared HF, 85% of people are unhappy in their jobs. That means 85% of the people who work in the USA hate their jobs. They hate their life's work! In turn, that means only 15% of people are engaged at work!

- According to the GOBankingRates 2019 annual survey, 69% of respondents said they have less than $1,000 in a savings account.

- In an article by Healthline, studies stated that more than two-thirds of adults in the United States are overweight or obese.

Mediocrity is a failing formula. At some point you need to find a reason to fight for more. For me and you, it is **THE FIGHT AGAINST MEDIOCRITY.**

I commend you for starting this book; that sets you apart. But that's just the beginning. Only a small portion of books are read past the first chapter (Or in this case chapter 0). I challenge you to commit to finishing this book. Anyone can start something, but winners finish. Will you commit to finishing this book and applying the principles in your life? If the answer is yes, then please sign the commitment pledge below.

I commit to reading "Talk Is Cheap – The Fight Against Mediocrity" and taking ferocious action to apply the principles it contains.

X: _____

Date: _____

**I promise that if you act on the principles contained in this book, you will have success and change your life forever.**

I hope you feel the intense desire to invite others to join this fight as well. I envision millions of people marching together with a common enemy and purpose. The enemy is mediocrity. The purpose is success and excellence. I want you to succeed and be excellent. I know you can do it; I believe in you. Welcome to THE FIGHT AGAINST MEDIOCRITY.

# CHAPTER 1

## 100% RESPONSIBILITY

**"Your life begins to change the day you take responsibility for it." —Steve Maraboli**

To have any type of success in life, realize that you are the only one responsible for the outcomes in your life. You are 100% responsible for everything that happens; The good, the bad, and the ugly—you're responsible for it all.

Where you are today is based on the decisions you made yesterday. Where you're going is determined by the decisions you make today and tomorrow. Where you were born, what your upbringing was like, how successful or unsuccessful your parents or relatives are, or anything else that has happened in your life up to this point does not determine your success. To control it, own it. The moment you point the finger of blame in any direction other than at the person in the mirror, you give away your power to change and improve. Think about that for a second: When you blame someone or something for an outcome, **you give them your power**. Once you've said, "It's not my fault; I don't control it," you no longer have the power to change. Humans are the only creatures with the power to determine their destiny: Your brain will listen and immediately stop looking for solutions once you point the finger of blame. By owning the problem, you are giving your brain the green light to find a solution to fix it. When you take responsibility for your problems, your brain will search high and low for a solution.

Even if it is legitimately someone else's fault, you must take responsibility. Otherwise, you give away your power to change. Arguably, the most important step toward any type of success in life is taking 100% responsibility.

The late Jim Rohn once said, "It's one of the highest forms of full maturity, accepting responsibility. It's the day you know you've passed from childhood to adulthood." I wonder if he was referencing the apostle St. Paul in 1 Corinthians 13:11 (KJV) when he taught the following, "When I was a child, I spake as a child, I understood as a child, I thought as a child: but when I became a man (or woman), I put away childish things." It's a childish instinct to blame others. A five-year-old can get away with that sort of behavior, but when an adult points across the room to a colleague and blames them for an unfinished project, it's, well, just plain pathetic.

## YOU, INC.

Life is so much sweeter when you take 100% responsibility for everything in your life. It's incredible to know that you're the CEO of You, Inc. No one is coming to save you. No one will believe in you more than *you*.

Years ago, I was on the road with the sales manager of one of the largest smart home companies in the world. I was pestering him to teach me everything he knew about selling and business. This guy had a blanket of confidence around him. Before he would knock on a door, he had already made up his mind that the family would become a client; there was no doubt in his mind. I asked him if he planned on selling door-to-door for his entire career, and he said something that I've never forgotten: "I'm not sure what I will do next, but I know whatever I do, my partners and I will CRUSH it."

I had never heard anyone speak with such certainty about business. It didn't feel like a cocky type of confidence. It was a surety he had of himself. A short while later, I began to understand why he was so confident. He had built a sales skill set that made him unstoppable. He knew he could create his own economy wherever he went, in whichever industry he chose. His skills gave him confidence that success in his career would always be within his control. That's the type of confidence you can have as you enter the top 1% of your field. You can have the confidence to create your economy wherever you go because of your acquired skills.

Even if you aren't a CEO, adopt the mindset of a CEO. In my first job out of college, I placed a sticky note on my computer screen that stated, "THINK LIKE AN OWNER." I felt it was crucial because I knew that the decisions I made wearing an "owner hat" were extremely different than those I'd make with an "employee hat." The owner looks to the future growth of the company, the bottom line, to world-class customer service, and improving systems and processes. I wanted to feel like the business was my baby just as much as it was the owner's. It's extremely difficult to do this, depending on your salary structure and job position. For instance, if you are a salaried employee with no defined bonus structure, then in the short term, it doesn't matter how much or how little you do. You'll still make the same amount of money. In the long run, this limited thinking will cost you your job and opportunities to grow in the company.

I've witnessed several of my friends make career decisions solely based on the amount of money they were going to make. Money shouldn't always be the motivating factor. Instead, ask yourself, "What skills will this opportunity teach me?" Sometimes it makes sense to take an opportunity because the experience will build skills that will result in higher returns in the future. Make thinking like an owner (the owner of You, Inc) a priority, and the long-term consequences will include increased pay, improved skill sets, and higher career satisfaction.

## DISCOURAGEMENT VS. DISCONTENT

As you start taking 100% responsibility for your life, you may feel discouraged: it can seem daunting. You're going to find several areas of your life where you are sick and tired of being sick and tired. Hold on to that feeling. It is the key to getting out of your current circumstances and moving toward change. As you begin to examine those feelings, there are two paths you can choose: discontentment or discouragement.

Discontentment is good. It's understanding that you aren't where you want to be, but that, with hard work and ferocious action, you can overcome any obstacle. Neal A. Maxwell said that divine discontent comes when we compare "what we are [to] what we have the power to become." If you are reading this book, I know you have big goals for your life, probably bigger than most of your peers'. This is typically accompanied by feelings of fear, doubt, uncertainty, and anxiety. That is normal. However, we are here to fight the normal. Be the 1% and fight those feelings head-on with relentless action, positive self-talk, and a desire to accomplish your goals so deep that it is downright scary. You know you are on the right track when people start commenting on how weird, strange, **obsessed,** optimistic, or different you are.

Discouragement, on the other hand, opens the floodgates for feelings of self-doubt, pity, and self-loathing. This is a bad mindset to maintain. Discouragement is destructive and paralyzing, and it breeds negativity. Being responsible for where you are will force you to realize that you've made some poor decisions. Welcome to the club. We all make bad choices, we all fall, and we all have areas we can improve. Breaking news: YOU ARE HUMAN! Don't let your circumstances define you: let them be the reason to change. It doesn't matter where you are or where you've been. What matters is what you are doing today and where that will lead you tomorrow.

## CHOOSING YOUR RESPONSE

As far back as I can remember, my dad would always say, "Kevin, you choose your response." I always thought he was unreasonable and naive. How could I withhold yelling at him when he wouldn't let me hang out with my friends past curfew, right? Well, not exactly. Psychologist Shahram Heshmat, PhD, says, "A person's emotional experience typically results from a subjective interpretation of an event, rather than from the event itself." In other words, your emotions come from your interpretation of what happens to you, not the actual event itself. Turns out my dad was right.

Some emotions are innate to the human condition. Emotions can be difficult to control, but you can manage how you respond to your emotions by the stories you create from an event.

Believe that things are happening for you, not to you. For instance, if your most profitable client decides to move to a competitor, your first thought might be, "Why is this happening to me? I must not have a very good business." Or you could choose a different response: "Now we have time to find an even more profitable client and look at different ways to improve our customer retention." The situation didn't change, but the responses were extremely different. Believe things are happening for you, not to you.

Acknowledging that, no matter the stimulus or event, you are responsible for your response, sets you free. It allows you to examine why you feel a certain way instead of blaming someone or something. It sounds great in practice, but it's extremely difficult to implement in your everyday life. We all have a carnal man or woman inside of us who is greedy, impatient, selfish, and prideful. We all get wound up and frustrated when things don't go our way, when a customer yells at us, and on and on. I find it extremely helpful to take a deep breath and examine my feelings. I ask myself, "Why am I feeling this way? What past experience is triggering this feeling? What can I control in this situation?"

## NEVER BE OFFENDED AGAIN

What people say to me, or about me, speaks more about their beliefs than it says about me. For example, after I married my wife, Lauren, a co-worker told me that I was now going to gain twenty pounds. Well, three years later, and not only have I not gained weight, but I'm also in the best shape of my life. What he was really saying is this, "I gained weight when I got married, so to justify my actions, I believe everyone will." It is like taking a weight off your shoulders when you realize that what people say discloses more about them than it does about you. Once I realized this, I started to smile when people criticized or insulted me. Why should I take it personally? As I said, they are saying more about themselves than they are about me. Emotionally unstable people have a strong tendency to bully and criticize others instead of dealing with their own problems. Smile at this criticism; it means you are moving the needle in the right direction.

## EMBRACE CRITICISM

When you start taking responsibility and pushing for positive change in your life, you will receive criticism. Congratulations! When you start receiving criticism, you know you are on the right path. The formula for success was given to us by Mahatma Gandhi when he said, "First they ignore you, then they laugh at you, then they fight you, then you win."

When you have a big dream or goal, you need attention so people know who you are and what you're doing. At first, you will be scared to share your dreams, and once you go all in, you will be laughed at and criticized by those who have given up on their dreams. Walt Disney was fired by a newspaper for "not being creative enough." He was later told that Mickey Mouse cartoons were "too scary for women." If that's not enough, "The Three Little Pigs" was rejected because it had only four characters. What if he would have quit because he was criticized?

As you continue to pound the pavement, the criticism will turn into hate. Once you've succeeded, you will be rewarded with admiration, usually by the same people who once criticized you.

As mentioned previously, the criticism says more about the giver than the receiver. Every person in history that has changed the world has always received crippling criticism. Think of Steve Jobs, Elon Musk, Martin Luther King Jr., Harriet Tubman, Henry Ford, and Jesus Christ. Elbert Hubbard said the following about criticism:

**"To avoid criticism, do nothing, say nothing, be nothing."**

Let that sink in. My greatest fear is that I will come to the end of my life only to look back and realize that I only reached a small portion of my potential because I was too afraid of failure and criticism. I am constantly working to be more like the type of person Steve Jobs described when he said the following:

> "Here's to the crazy ones. The misfits. The rebels. The troublemakers. The round pegs in the square holes. The ones who see things differently. They're not fond of rules. And they have no respect for the status quo. You can quote them, disagree with them, glorify or vilify them. About the only thing you can't do is ignore them. Because they change things. They push the human race forward. While some see them as the crazy ones, we see genius. Because the people who are crazy enough to think they can change the world, are the ones who do."

## NO EXCUSES

Taking 100% responsibility is the first ingredient of success. Owning everything about your life gives your mind permission to create solutions. To control it, you must own it. Use the words "I choose" to feel the power of accountability. Avoid spending time with people who blame and criticize others. Write down circumstances in your life that you want to change and own them. Own everything, even if it isn't your fault. This type of mindset will not come naturally. It takes intentional effort, but it is worth it. If you choose to take 100% responsibility for your life, your mindset will automatically be among the top 1%. The late Kobe Bryant said, "I have nothing in common with lazy people who blame others for their lack of success. Great things come from hard work and perseverance. No excuses."

## REAL-LIFE EXAMPLES OF 100% RESPONSIBILITY

It's helpful to see real-life examples of situations where you're tempted to point the finger of blame or make excuses. Let's look at some of those situations.

**1.** **"I'm late to work because of the horrible traffic."**

Traffic is easy to blame when you're late; we've all blamed the traffic. Traffic sucks, but it is not the reason you're late. Poor planning and preparation are the cause of lateness. One solution is to wake up before everyone else and beat the traffic.

I worked for one of the largest real estate developers in Utah after graduating college. They are headquartered in Salt Lake City, Utah, and during the high-traffic hours of the day, my commute was about an hour. I learned very quickly that the traffic was unpredictable starting at 7:00 a.m. It could be forty-five minutes to the office, or it could be an hour and a half, depending on traffic. So, I had two choices: be late most of the time or wake up early and go to a gym near my office so I could control the outcome. I could not control the traffic, but I *could* control what time I woke up. I was always on time because I chose to control my circumstances and not blame the traffic. Had I continued to blame the traffic, my mind would have stopped looking for solutions to the problem and simply accepted mediocrity.

## 2. "I can never get my body in shape."

What scares me most about this statement is that the moment this leaves your lips, the brain stops looking for solutions to help your body. The brain waves the white flag, and it creates a downward spiral. Let's face it: everyone wants a six-pack, but no one wants to sweat at the gym every day. I promise you don't have to be Arnold Schwarzenegger to find a workout program and follow it. My best advice would be to get a coach who can teach you and hold you accountable. It requires a mindset shift. To get in shape physically, first get your mind in shape and believe you can change.

### 3. "I don't have time."

Everyone receives the same twenty-four hours. You don't "have the time," you "make the time." One of the most eye-opening activities you can perform is to track your time for one week. Try it. Track every minute to see where you spend your time. I guarantee you can *make* time to chase your dreams. We each are given the same twenty-four hours, 1,440 minutes, 86,400 seconds. How you spend it will determine your future.

### 4. "I can't afford it."

If you use this phrase, you will always be right. Instead, ask this question: "How can I afford it?" This question opens the mind to look for solutions and possibilities. The first statement closes the mind and encourages a scarcity mindset. There is an abundant amount of money and resources in the world. There is only a lack of people who are willing to go get them.

**5.** "That person was born like that. I just wasn't born with XYZ skill set."

Anyone can do anything they set their mind to with enough time and practice. Most people who have a "natural ability" set aside hundreds of hours until it became natural. Will Smith is famous for saying the following: "The only thing that I see that is distinctly different about me is I'm not afraid to die on a treadmill. I will not be outworked, period. You might have more talent than me, you might be smarter than me, you might be sexier than me . . . But if we get on the treadmill together, there are two things: You're getting off first, or I'm going to die." Michelangelo, arguably one of the greatest artists in history, said, "If people knew how hard I worked to get my mastery, it wouldn't seem so wonderful at all." Hard work and consistency will always defy the odds.

**6.** "I *have* to."

At first glance, it may seem like an error classifying this statement as an excuse, but it's all about your mindset. Try saying the following instead to shift your paradigm toward success: "I *get/choose* to." Say it out loud: "I *choose* to." Say it to yourself over and over again. Go ahead, try it right now. Do you feel accountability rushing through your veins? I do this all the time to enforce 100% responsibility in my life. You don't *have* to do anything. Sure, there will be consequences for your choices, but you are not forced to do anything. Saying that you "have" to go to work, finish the project, or talk to a prospect is just not true! We choose how we spend our time and resources, consciously or unconsciously.

**7.** **"What if I offend someone? What if they don't like me?"**

I like to call this *pleasing people paralysis*--PPP, if you will. We all know that person (or are that person) who is always stressed to the max about what other people think or say. I hope this doesn't boggle your mind too much: **PEOPLE DON'T CARE!** Eleanor Roosevelt once said, "You wouldn't worry so much about what others think of you if you realized how seldom they do." Most people are so absorbed in the world between their own two ears that they never even see what you do or don't do. In fact, as was already mentioned, those who *do* get offended or don't like you are actually reflecting more about themselves.

Steve Jobs said the following about overcoming fear, and I relate it to overcoming PPP, when he said, "Remembering that I'll be dead soon is the most important tool I've ever encountered to help me make the big choices in life.

All fear of embarrassment or failure—these things just fall away in the face of death, leaving only what is truly important."

Now let me just clarify, this isn't a free pass to be a jerk just because it doesn't matter what people think. It gives you permission to do something that pushes the envelope of what was previously impossible. It permits you to be true to yourself as well as to your goals and dreams.

**8.** **"It is what it is."**

When Henry Ford decided to produce his famous V-8 motor, he chose to build an engine with the entire eight cylinders cast in one block. The design was placed on paper, but the engineers declared that it was simply impossible to cast an eight-cylinder engine block in one piece. Ford replied, "Produce it anyway." They figured it out and create the world's first eight-cylinder engine block in one piece. The lesson is to be unreasonable and never accept that "it is what it is." Ignore the naysayers, because, like Nelson Mandela once said, "It always seems impossible until it's done."

## 9. "I didn't know ..."

This has been the most difficult for me to overcome. I find myself wanting to blame ignorance. I recently received a call notifying me that I made a mistake. My mind immediately went to the excuse, "It's not my fault. I didn't know." As I was about to blurt out my sinful statement, I realized that, if I blamed ignorance, I would immediately let my mind relax and not take responsibility. I wouldn't learn, and I wouldn't remember the knowledge as well as if I took 100% responsibility.

### VICTIM VS. VILLAIN

The language you use when you are making this life-altering mental shift is crucial. The brain is a truth-seeking machine. Whatever you tell yourself, the brain will look for ways to validate your beliefs. For example, if you continually tell yourself that you are bad at math, then your brain will keep looking for ways to prove that you are, indeed, bad at math. You are the victim, and math becomes the villain. How you phrase the circumstances of your life will make a huge difference in your behavior. In the traffic example, instead of saying, "I'm late because of the traffic," use the phrase, "Until now ... but now ..." It goes like this, "**Until now** I've been late because of the traffic, **but now** I wake up earlier and go to the gym, so the traffic isn't a problem." I learned this from one of my mentors, Jeff Shore. It is a brilliant way to break out of the victim/villain mentality and take responsibility for your circumstances. Instead of trapping yourself in a belief box, the phrase "But now . . ." allows you to change and never be a victim again.

## NOTHING CHANGES UNLESS SOMETHING CHANGES

The most successful people in the world commit quickly. The definition of *commitment* is "the state or quality of being dedicated to a cause, activity, etc." I can immediately spot a successful, committed individual because, instead of saying, "I'll get around to it," they immediately pull out their calendars and schedule it into their lives. They are committed, no ifs, ands, or buts.

Tony Robbins says, "Contrary to popular wisdom, knowledge is not power, it's potential power. Knowledge is not mastery. Execution is mastery. Execution will trump knowledge every day of the week."

Each chapter ends with action items you can complete today. I promise that, as you act, you will see results. The action items for Chapter 1 are below.

Would you like additional help and motivation? Scan the QR code to access free resources including my favorite motivational videos.

**CHAPTER ONE - 100% RESPONSIBILITY**

# TAKE ACTION
## NOTHING CHANGES UNLESS SOMETHING CHANGES

- Look at yourself in the mirror and say out loud, "I take 100% responsibility for where I'm at today."
- List your excuse areas and use the "Until Now... But Now..." framework to overcome your victim mentality.
- Use the phrase "I choose to..." instead of "I have to..."
- Set a goal to **become the top 1% in your industry**. Who is currently in the top 1%? Reach out to them and ask if you can interview them for thirty minutes. Implement what they teach you immediately.

# FREE
# ADDITIONAL
# RESOURCES

SCAN ME

or visit TheFightAgainstMediocrity.com/Resources to download an editable PDF of the action items.

# CHAPTER 2

## BELIEF

**"Limits, like fears, are often just an illusion." —Michael Jordan**

I recently purchased a Ford F-150, and while completing the purchase, the salesperson taught my wife and me about the features of the truck. We were excited and eager to learn. He described a feature called MyKey that was very intriguing to me. Essentially, it allows the owner of the truck to set up safety preferences for each key fob. It is intended to regulate teen driving by limiting speed, controlling preferences for Traction Control, 911 Assist, Do Not Disturb, and audio volume. It is a governor, which is not a new concept in vehicles and machinery. The salesperson emphasized that, once engaged, it is extremely tricky for customers to turn off. He told a story of a man who unknowingly activated MyKey to limit his truck speed to 60 MPH. The man called the salesperson in a rage, shouting, "You sold me a lemon!" He was driving down a Texas back road, and the truck wouldn't pass 60 MPH.

This story got me thinking about the governors we impose on our minds and how difficult they are to remove and change. We each have preferences, experiences, ideas, music, books, videos, friends, and family who have shaped our beliefs about who we are and what we can or cannot do. The irony is that we are often like the person yelling at the sales agent for installing them, when, in reality, it is our own responsibility to recognize them and make the necessary changes. You set internal governors on how much you can achieve. You want to achieve above your governors, but until you change the settings on your "MyKey", self-image, and/or belief, you will never achieve it. You can press on the gas all day long, but until the engine (your mind) is reprogrammed, it is a moot point.

The achievement of a goal or desire is **led by belief**. It isn't the other way around. Believe it is possible in your mind and then you will be able to achieve it in reality.

## PLASTIC SURGERY AND SELF-IMAGE

Maxwell Maltz, the author of *Psycho-Cybernetics*, started as a plastic surgeon and saw the amazing and detrimental effects plastic surgery has on a person's self-image. Self-image, as Maxwell describes it, is the "mental blueprint or picture of ourselves." The beliefs you have about yourself typically stem from your experiences, both good and bad, you've had in life and your reactions to those experiences. In Maltz's words, "Once an idea or a belief about ourselves goes into this picture (self-belief), it becomes "true," as far as we personally are concerned. We do not question its validity, but proceed to act upon it *just as if it were true.*"

You are walking around with self-beliefs that control what you do and how you see yourself, and they may not even be true! The worst part is that these beliefs could be holding you back just like the MyKey did for the Texan who couldn't accelerate past 60 MPH. The good news for you is that you can change your self-image by who you spend time with and what content you consume on a daily basis.

To illustrate, I will share two stories from Maxwell's book. The first is of a young boy who was ridiculed because his ears were too big and was even called "a taxicab with both doors open." Once this boy had surgery, he no longer felt humiliated. He eventually became a successful executive. The surgery only changed his physical appearance, but it was enough for him to change his self-image and live according to new beliefs. Before you think that the moral of the story is to go get plastic surgery, let me share another story.

A woman with a large bump on her nose, who had lived an unsure and bashful life, also had plastic surgery. Unlike the young boy whose life turned around for the better, the woman's life went unchanged post-surgery. She continued to live an anxious and awkward life. Although she had a "new face," she continued wearing the same old personality. Her self-image went unchanged, and so did her behavior. It all starts with how you see yourself on the inside, and that projects on your external life.

Darren Hardy calls this phenomenon the "You Factor." He states, "It's important to understand that you don't get in life what you want; **you get in life what you are**." The alarming statistics of divorce rates after the first marriage illustrate this point. In an article written by Mark Banschick, MD, he writes, "Statistics have shown that in the U.S . . . . 67 percent of second and 73 percent of third marriages end in divorce." It makes sense when you realize that the person left the relationship but took their bad habits with them to the next marriage. "They didn't address the real problem," Darren says. "The same set of circumstances and patterns of behavior will create the same outcome over and over again." You have to change you! You must become more to do more.

## BABY ELEPHANT SYNDROME

I'll share one more illustration of how self-beliefs are limiting your abilities: It is called *baby elephant syndrome*. When elephants are young, they are frequently trained for the circus or are kept as attractions. The trainer takes the young elephant, who weighs about two hundred pounds, and ties its feet together with either a rope or a metal clasp. The young elephant's initial instincts are to escape and roam free in the wild. As the elephant thrusts a few steps forward, it is jerked back by the rope. After a few more attempts and a bloody ankle, the elephant slowly accepts its defeat and the new reality that it cannot escape. Fast-forward a few years, and this same elephant weighs up to ten thousand pounds and is twelve feet long. You can rest assured that, at this point, the elephant has graduated the ankle tie to something substantially larger to keep it from fleeing, right? Surprisingly, no. The same ankle rope or metal clasp is still used to hold this enormous mammal. The elephant's mind has been conditioned to believe that it cannot escape. Despite the fact that the elephant can push over a tree with its trunk, the mental barrier created years earlier holds the elephant hostage.

Humans aren't much different than elephants. You have beliefs that were created years ago that hold you back, and they are just as ridiculous as a small rope holding a gigantic elephant back. To break free from their grasp, they must first be identified and acknowledged. It takes hard work and self-reflection to identify and break these limiting beliefs. Ask your friends and family if they can identify any of them for you. Pay particular attention to what you say.

Have you ever said, "I can't afford that?" That phrase comes from the false belief that there is a lack of money in the world, which is false. Your mind creates excuses for why you haven't achieved your goals. Once you've identified a false belief, it's important to find the correct belief, so you can replace the weeds of wrong thinking with the flowers of fundamental truth.

About two years ago, I went to Thailand and was able to see trained elephants. Sure enough, they were tied on just one leg and did not try to break free. They will live their entire life this way. If you don't take time to get to the root of your false beliefs, you will remain tied down for the rest of your life as well.

## CREATIVE IMAGINATION

Maltz explains that we are goal-seeking "servo-mechanisms." Whether steering us in the direction of our goals or working to solve problems in our path, our brains and nervous systems strive to guide us in the direction of our goals and desires. Just like a bird instinctively knows how to make a nest or fly south for the winter, even though it was born in the spring, our minds automatically find a way to serve our goals and dreams. Each animal has the goal of self-preservation and procreation. They are wired to instinctively succeed in those goals. However, humans have something no animal has: *creative imagination*. Man is not just a creature, but a creator. Glenn Clark, the author of *The Man Who Tapped the Secrets of the Universe*, said, "Imagination of all man's faculties is the most God-like."

Everything that has been created or accomplished in the world has followed the law of two creations: The first creation is in the mind, and the second creation is in reality. Stephen Covey demonstrates this message in his best-selling book *The Seven Habits of Highly Effective People*. In his list of habits to become more effective, habit two is "Begin with the end in mind," which Stephen likens to constructing a home. I am very familiar with this process, and I've found that a home is typically "built" on paper at least seven times before a shovel ever hits the dirt. By the time the home starts, everyone involved has visualized the details of construction, the hundreds of products and trade contractors involved, and the final outcome. If done correctly, there should be no doubt that it can be done, and accomplishment is only a matter of time and effort.

In an interview, pop star Usher mentioned that, ever since he was a child, he imagined performing in front of thousands of people. He *believed* it was a reality way before it ever *became* reality. Arnold Schwarzenegger won the Mr. Olympia title in his mind while training in the gym long before he ever held the trophy in reality. The list goes on and on. If you can create it in your mind, then given the right amount of effort you can create it in real life. The opposite is also true. Unbelief leads to quitting or never even starting.

All of the most successful people in the world, the top 1% of people in every category have one thing in common: they have a strong belief that they can and will win. That doesn't mean they don't have setbacks, disappointments, failures, and doubts, because they do. They put this to one side and focus on what they can control (hint, hint, Chapter 1) and use visualization to make their goals a reality. Don't take my word for it; take their word for it.

- "Impossible is not a fact, it's an opinion." —Tony Robbins
- "If you can see it here (mind), and you have the courage enough to speak it, it will happen." —Conor McGregor
- "Just because it's never been done, doesn't mean it can't be done." —Robin Sharma
- "Whether you think you can, or you think you can't, you are usually right." —Abe Lincoln
- "Your net worth is directly proportional to your self-worth." —Jim Rohn

- "One of the reasons so many people don't have what they want in life is that their level of belief isn't high enough to attract it." —Bryan Dodge

- "If you hear a voice within you say 'you cannot paint,' then by all means paint, and that voice will be silenced." —Vincent van Gogh

- "If we all did the things we are capable of doing, we would literally astound ourselves." —Thomas Alva Edison

- "Our deepest fear is not that we are inadequate. Our deepest fear is that we are powerful beyond measure. It is our light, not our darkness, that most frightens us. We ask ourselves, 'Who am I to be brilliant, gorgeous, talented, fabulous?' Actually, who are you not to be?" —Marianne Williamson

- "Successful people have fear, successful people have doubts, and successful people have worries. They just don't let these feelings stop them." —T. Harv Eker

- "You can have anything you want if you are willing to give up the belief that you can't have it." —Dr. Robert Anthony

- "Inaction breeds doubt and fear. Action breeds confidence and courage. If you want to conquer fear, do not sit home and think about it. Go out and get busy." —Dale Carnegie

- "Nothing can stop the man with the right mental attitude from achieving his goal; nothing on earth can help the man with the wrong mental attitude." —Thomas Jefferson

- "If you are insecure, guess what? The rest of the world is too. Do not overestimate the competition and underestimate yourself. You are better than you think." — T. Harv Eker

- "The moment you doubt whether you can fly, you cease forever to be able to do it." —J. M. Barrie

- "We avoid the things that we're afraid of because we think there will be dire consequences if we confront them. But the truly dire consequences in our lives come from avoiding things that we need to learn about or discover." —Shakti Gawain

- "Man often becomes what he believes himself to be. If I keep on saying to myself that I cannot do a certain thing, it is possible that I may end up really becoming incapable of doing it. On the contrary, if I shall have the belief that I can do it, I shall surely acquire the capacity to do it, even if I may not have it at the beginning." —Mahatma Gandhi

- "The outer conditions of a person's life will always be found to reflect their inner beliefs." —James Allen

- "Your chances of success in any undertaking can always be measured by your belief in yourself." —Robert Collier

- "The thing always happens that you really believe in; and the belief in a thing makes it happen." —Frank Lloyd Wright

- "Some things have to be believed to be seen!" —Ralph Hodgson
- "Man is made by his belief. As he believes, so he is." — Johann Wolfgang von Goethe

## WHEN SOMEONE TELLS YOU IT'S IMPOSSIBLE

One of the greatest stories of belief is that of Roger Banister. Sir Roger Gilbert Bannister was a British athlete and neurologist who ran the first sub-four-minute mile. At the time, science  suggested that a sub-four-minute mile was *physically impossible.* They said that, if someone did it, they would collapse, dead! Imagine that for a moment: Medical experts were telling people that running a sub-four-minute mile was impossible, and Roger Banister still tried it.

Roger said in an interview that Sweden believed it could not be done, so they gave up. They didn't give up physically until they gave up mentally. John Landy had run four minutes and two seconds several times and said that there seemed to be a brick wall at that point. Roger felt like it was possible to shave a few seconds off of Landy's time and that the sub-four-minute mile could be accomplished. He believed it was possible in his mind first, and then the impossible happened.

On the morning of May 6, 1954, at the age of twenty-five, Roger Bannister broke not only a world record, but also a mental barrier that changed the world forever. He charged over the finish line with a time of 3:59.4. There were only about 1,200 people in attendance that day, but the minds of millions were reconstructed to believe that the sub-four-minute mile was possible.

Something that isn't mentioned in most accounts of Roger Bannister's world-breaking race are the unfavorable circumstances of that day. There was a fifteen-mile-an-hour crosswind during the race. It was said that, without the wind, many believe Roger could have been closer to 3:58. Roger said that there **"comes a moment when you have to accept the weather and have an all-out effort and I decided today was the day."** Roger took 100% responsibility for his circumstances. He could have blamed the weather before the race began and waved the white flag in his mind, but he didn't.

What have you been told is impossible? What have you told yourself is impossible? The obstacles we face in life are like brick walls in our paths. The brick walls are meant to keep people out who don't want to fight for what is on the other side. But there is always a way through, around, or over the brick wall. It is there not to keep you out, but rather to present an opportunity to show how badly you want something. How will you break down the mental barriers and reach your sub-four-minute mile? Take some time now to write down the brick walls that have mentally blocked you from accomplishing your goals. Visualize yourself overcoming each one of them and believe it is possible. Then make a plan and take action immediately!

## MR. OLYMPIA

Belief and confidence start in the mind with positive self-talk. Everything you tell yourself, read, listen to, watch, and think about turns into your self-image. These things shape your beliefs about life and yourself. You are nothing more than the sum of all you've thought, read, listened to, and watched.

For the last six years, I have listened to motivational videos on YouTube nearly every day because I want my self-image to reflect that anything is possible.

My favorite videos feature Arnold Schwarzenegger and his incredible journey. When he was just a young boy, he had a vision and dream of coming to America and becoming a bodybuilding champion.

When he lifted weights, people would ask him why he smiled while everyone around him looked angry when they lifted weights at the gym. He said the following:

> "To me, I am shooting for a goal. In front of me is the Mr. Universe title. So every rep that I do gets me closer to accomplishing that goal. To make this goal, this vision, a reality. Every single set that I do, every repetition of weight that I lift will get me a step closer to turning this goal into a reality. So I couldn't wait to do another five hundred-pound squat. I couldn't wait to do another five hundred-pound bench press. I couldn't wait to do another two thousand sit-ups. I couldn't wait for the next exercise. So let me tell you that visualizing your goal and going after it makes it fun. You have to have a purpose no matter what you do in life."

Arnold cultivated a skill that you must develop if you hope to conquer your goals. He was relentless in visualizing and believing in his goal. He believed it was already his for the taking. He didn't see any reason why, if he believed and put in the work, he couldn't be Mr. Olympia, the highest-paid actor in the world, or the governor of California. He went on to do all those things! It was so clear in his mind that nothing or no one could stop him.

In his book *You Can Become the Person You Want to Be*, Robert H. Schuller said, **"What goals would you be setting for yourself if you knew you could not fail?"**

Belief in yourself, your goals, and your future potential are necessary elements of being able to get what you want in life. You can do it! Say it out loud: "I can do it." I'm rooting for you. I know you can win The Fight Against Mediocrity.

## ELEVATE YOUR SIGHTS

I've learned from dozens of the best real estate developers in the United States, and I've noticed something that makes the biggest developers stand apart from the rest. It's a secret that they don't want me to share with you because it's how they get the biggest projects that make the most profit. Are you ready for this gold nugget of knowledge? Okay, here it is: *They think bigger.* By thinking bigger, they make more money and typically do the same amount of work as smaller developers. All the big developers say something like, "It takes the same amount of work to do a 10-lot subdivision as it does to do a 250-lot subdivision." Think about it: you complete the same steps for each project, but one is twenty-five times larger and significantly more profitable. Each project requires working with an engineer, a bank, a city council, a staff, and a construction team. The only difference is in the developers' level of thinking and belief in themselves to complete the bigger project.

Belief is a crucial step, but so is expecting more of yourself. You must raise your goals and raise your standards. Tony Robbins says, "You don't get in life what you want. You get in life what you expect. You must raise your standards." I promise you will be constantly tempted to think small and aim for small goals; that's why it's a *fight*!

If you don't believe in yourself, believe in the words of Steve Jobs: "Everything around you that you call life was made up by people that were no smarter than you. And you can change it, you can influence it . . . Once you learn that, you'll never be the same."

Need motivation and more help? Scan the QR code to access free resources including my favorite motivational videos.

**CHAPTER TWO - BELIEF**

# TAKE ACTION
## NOTHING CHANGES UNLESS SOMETHING CHANGES

- Ask yourself, "What goals would I be setting for myself if I knew I could not fail?" Write them down.
- Build self-belief by doing the following for your goals:
  a. Write them down in present tense twice every day.
  b. Say them out loud in the present tense.
  c. Visualize all five senses of what it will be like once you've accomplished the goal.
  d. Make a plan w/ daily, weekly, and monthly checkpoints.
  e. Take action NOW!

# FREE
## ADDITIONAL
## RESOURCES

SCAN ME

or visit TheFightAgainstMediocrity.com/Resources
to download an editable PDF of the action items.

# CHAPTER 3

# HARD WORK

**"Nothing works unless you do." —Arnold Schwarzenegger**

*Work*, as defined by Merriam Webster, is the following:

a. To perform or carry through a task requiring **sustained effort or continuous repeated operations**

b. To exert oneself physically or mentally especially in **sustained effort for a purpose** or under compulsion or necessity

c. To produce a desired effect or result

Work is the bridge from where you are now to where you want to be. There is no shortcut, detour, magic pill, or back door. Anyone who is in the top 1% of their field is there because of hard work. Don't fool yourself. My grandpa constantly tells me, "To achieve your goals, there is no way around hard, hard, work."

Hard work is at the very core of #TalkIsCheap. Hard work is what turns a talker into an achiever. Nothing good has ever come to fruition without hard work. No joy or satisfaction comes without hard work. The Fight Against Mediocrity is won by wielding the sword of hard work.

## LIFE IS A MOVING RIVER

Life is an upstream battle. Life is like a moving river: sometimes it moves fast, and sometimes it moves so calmly that you hardly notice it is pushing you along. It depends on the stage of life you are in. The important thing to note is that, no matter how fast life is pushing against you, you must swim upstream. It is impossible to stay the same person you were yesterday. **You are either moving forward or backward.** You are either pushing upstream or drifting downstream. You can never stay in the same spot.

That is where the mediocre workers get crushed in life. They think that their jobs are safe, and life is good, so they just coast through the same routine, never pushing. The next thing they know, they are unneeded and outdated. Does the phrase, "Eat, drink, and be merry, for tomorrow we die" sound familiar? This is the motto of the mediocre. If you don't believe me, watch as, in the upcoming years, technology continues to eliminate millions of jobs. For instance, there are cashiers who assumed that their jobs were always safe and are now dumbfounded that they are obsolete. If you choose to drift with the current of mediocrity, you are making a choice to become obsolete in the future. The river of life is always moving and is no respecter of persons. It will treat you and the person next to you the exact same way.

## JUST START

My wife, Lauren, recently lost her AirPods as she was about to leave for the gym. If you own a pair of AirPods, you know the thought of losing them is unbearable. We looked for nearly a half hour, tearing the house apart. We couldn't find them anywhere! The last place she remembered having them was at my parents' house, so we went there and, you guessed it, tore it apart. We didn't have any success. The next day she had accepted the reality that her AirPods were gone. A devastating reality to live in. She decided to go to the gym without them, and as she put on a shoe, she felt something inside her shoe. Would you like to guess what it was? Yes, it was her AirPods!

This story carries a very crucial life lesson. Sometimes in life, you won't start something because you don't feel like you have all the resources or knowledge you need (like

AirPods). Start anyway! You will end up finding most of what you need after you start, not before. No amount of preparation will compensate for taking the plunge into the unknown.

## DON'T WAIT UNTIL YOU ARE COMPENSATED

Larry Miller is a legend in the state of Utah. Larry Miller made his billions from owning car dealerships, movie theaters, a Minor League Baseball team, and the NBA Utah Jazz basketball team. Aside from his billionaire status, he is known for the good he did in his community. One of his most memorable acts is saving the Utah Jazz from leaving the state of Utah in 1985. He did this by securing $10 million two minutes before the purchase deadline. It was a tremendous feat and one that Utah has been extremely grateful for.

According to his autobiography, Miller had been lied to and mistreated by not one, not two, not three, not four, but five of his employers! He had always outperformed (way outperformed) his peers while working in car part stores and was continually promised more money, but the employer continued to go back on his word. One day, he discovered he did 65% of the work in a parts store while all the other employees put together did the other 35%. Regardless of his performance, the other employees got paid more because of their tenure: The policy stated that each employee would receive a nickel raise every ninety days, and Miller hadn't been there as long as his coworkers.

One day, Miller asked his boss for a quarter raise. He was getting married soon and needed the extra money. His boss denied him the raise, so Larry was determined that if they were only going to pay him $1.35, he would only give them $1.35 worth of work. Later that night, Larry joined his grandfather for dinner and told him about the predicament. His grandfather taught him a principle that changed Larry's life. He said,

"You could do exactly that and still perform at such a high level that you would outperform your coworkers. So they would never know you were giving less than you had. But you would know, and frankly, **you would be the only guy to be hurt by your underperformance**. So, as your grandpa, I am going to promise you that as long as you continue to take their paycheck, if you work as hard as you can and learn all that you can in that business, someday it will pay off many times over."

The prophecy was fulfilled. Larry purchased his first car dealership when he was thirty-five years old, and the rest is history.

Most people don't work hard because they don't feel like they make enough money to justify the work. They do enough to get by because, "hey, that's the amount I get paid to do." Then the cycle continues. This is one of the great paradoxes of life. You don't wait to work hard once you start earning what you are worth. You work hard to be worthy of being paid what you're worth and hopefully more. **Work always comes before wealth.**

The effort you put forth today in your education, self-improvement, and mindset will pay dividends in the future. The work you put in today will bear fruit in the future. That's why so many people only put in the work temporarily: They don't see immediate results, get impatient, and then stop altogether. The most successful people keep going, keep pushing, and keep growing *every single day*.

## DON'T TAKE SHORTCUTS

Kobe Bryant is the model of hard work. Anyone who says Kobe was born a basketball legend has not witnessed his work ethic. He's known for saying, "Rest at the end, not in the middle." When you quit in the middle, you are only cheating yourself.

During one trip to China, Kobe hosted a basketball training camp and promised all the participants a free pair of shoes if they completed the drills. One participant was half a foot shy from reaching the required line during one of the drills. Kobe stopped the entire camp and forced him to run three suicides (A suicide consists of running to a line on the floor, running back to the original starting point, then running slightly further than the previous line and back to the starting point again until the entire length of the court is covered). Kobe wanted to make sure that he and everyone in attendance understood that you rest at the end, not in the middle.

Kobe Bryant talked about "doing the math" on hard work: if you want to be better at whatever you do, put in the work. If you put in twenty hours per week and the competition only works five, you have the upper hand. Simple math. If you want to widen the gap between the new you and the old you, put in more time more consistently.

## THE SWEAT RULE

I once learned that if you're not sweating, you're not working. I found that statement fascinating, and I've taken it to heart. I love sweat: it is physical proof that I'm working hard. I'm not talking about a little sweat either. I'm talking about sweat so intense I can wring my shirt out and fill a cup. If you go to the gym and give minimal work, you'll get minimal results. On the other hand, if you go to the gym and go all out, the results will arrive ten times faster. I often see people who start going to the gym and complain that they aren't seeing any results. My advice is always *go harder*. Give 110% while you are at the gym. You will live with the effort you put in for the rest of the day. When I leave the gym knowing I gave my all, that fuels everything else I do the rest of the day. This principle applies to everything in life. If you want to see results faster, go harder and *break a sweat!*

## THERE IS NO MAGIC PILL

There is no way to shortcut hard work. You can fake it for a short time, but eventually, the results will always tell the true story.

When I was young, my mother forced me to take piano lessons. Looking back, I wish I had taken them more seriously, but hindsight is always 20/20. I would rarely practice, and during my weekly lessons, I would fumble my way over the keys like Bambi learning to run. It sounded like tossing a pan down stairs. My teacher would always get notably frustrated due to my lack of effort. I always felt like I could get away with this until the recital came along. The recital was the coliseum that would tell the true story of each student's efforts. I'm sure I embarrassed my parents as I fumbled through the keys of my recital piece. It was as if it was the first time I'd played a piano.

The moral of the story is that, over time, whatever you do in the dark will always show in the light. You can try to take the shortcuts, the silver bullets, or the magic pills, but time will always tell the true story. We reap what we sow. This principle is as old as the sun is bright. In Galatians 6:7 (KJV), we learn, "Be not deceived; God is not mocked: for whatsoever a man soweth, that shall he also reap."

## MUHAMMED ALI

Arnold Schwarzenegger said the following about Muhammed Ali:

> **"Muhammed Ali worked his butt off, and I saw it firsthand. I remember that there was a sportswriter in the gym when Ali was working out doing sit-ups and he asked Ali, "How many sit-ups do you do?" And he said, "I don't start counting until it hurts."**

Muhammed Ali's work ethic is not unique among high achievers. The mistake most people make is that, when they see Muhammed in the ring, dominating his opponent, they think he was born a winner. They trick themselves into thinking that he is successful, not because of hard work, but because he is gifted. World-class status takes hard work. It will start with the phrase, "I don't start counting until it hurts."

The trick high achievers tap into is that they *enjoy* the hard work. They enjoy it because they know the **payment of hard work is success**.

Elon Musk would sleep in his office and shower at the YMCA when he started his first company. He only had one computer, so he coded all night to ensure the website was live during the day. At the time of this writing, Elon Musk is the richest person in the world. He is wealthy because he works extremely hard. Some of you might think his genius is responsible for his success, but everyone knows a prodigy who only talks about their ideas and doesn't back them up with hard, hard work. They never move further than the couch. Elon Musk once said about his goals, "I don't ever give up. I'd either have to be dead or incapacitated." Are you willing to take the same stance as you pursue your goals and dreams?

## DO IT NOW!

Brian Tracy is known for encouraging vocal positive affirmations. He said that, each morning, you should wake up and repeat the phrase, "Do it now," ten times. When you feel compelled to procrastinate, the words, "Do it now," will encourage you to complete the task quickly.

**"If you want to make an easy job seem mighty hard, just keep putting off doing it." —Olin Miller**

Nothing in life works unless you do. Most people are trained to complete tasks that are urgent. Some of those urgent tasks are important, and some are not. Most people procrastinate the tasks that are **very important, but not urgent**. The urgent tasks beg for our attention, while the very important and not urgent tasks get buried under piles of paperwork.

Important and not urgent are the tasks that have the greatest impact on your future, but a very low impact on today. These include reading, exercising, eating healthily, spending time with family, etc. The longer you put these tasks to one side, the more urgent they will become until you are forced to take care of them. A great example is health. Many top executives and business owners are known for their incredible work ethics, but because taking care of their bodies is not urgent, they don't make it a priority. Then, one day, they wake up with health problems that cost them significant time, energy, and stress, which are now incredibly urgent problems. Implement the "do it now" mentality on those important and not urgent tasks.

## THE SECOND PLACE MENTALITY

Once you have had some success in life, it is extremely tempting to bask in the victories of previous achievements. Nothing kills success like success. Strive to have the mentality that you are in second place. Never allow past success to overshadow future potential. No one wants to hear about what you did or didn't do in high school. Complacency is a cancer that plagues the Fight Against Mediocrity.

Everything you have and everything you are depends on your choices. It is as simple as that. To change what you have and who you are, change your daily choices. Choose to work hard. I promise you will never look back at your life and regret working hard.

Need motivation and more help? Scan the QR code to access free resources including my favorite motivational videos.

**CHAPTER THREE - HARD WORK**

# TAKE ACTION
## NOTHING CHANGES UNLESS SOMETHING CHANGES

- Never leave the gym until you're sweating.
- Don't wait until you get a pay raise to work hard. Follow Larry's grandpa's advice: "If you work as hard as you can and learn all that you can in that business (your current role), **someday it will pay off many times over.**"
- **Just start.** I promise you'll figure it out along the way.
- Smile while you work. Each rep gets you closer to your goal.
- Don't talk about past success. **Show today's work.**

# FREE
# ADDITIONAL
# RESOURCES

**SCAN ME**

or visit TheFightAgainstMediocrity.com/Resources
to download an editable PDF of the action items.

# CHAPTER 4

## CRUSH THE MORNING

**"Mornings are a God-given gift to the high achiever." — Kevin Kartchner**

Kobe Bryant is one of the greatest basketball players of all time, not only because of his innate abilities, but because of his extraordinary work ethic, mindset, and discipline. When Kobe accepted the Icon Award at the ESPYs in 2016, he said the following: "We're not on this stage just because of talent or ability. We're up here because of 4:00 a.m."

What is so important about 4:00 a.m.? What is so important about waking up early in the morning? Will it really make a difference in your life? Let me answer that for you: **YES, IT WILL!** The Fight Against Mediocrity starts in the early hours of the morning. The adversary is still asleep, and as a warrior, you can get a massive strategic advantage over your opponent. Kobe Bryant outlines this extremely well in an interview at TEDxShanghai quoted below:

"If your job is to try to be the best basketball player you can be. To do that you have to practice, you have to train, right? You want to train as much as you can, as often as you can. So, if you get up at 10:00 in the morning, train at 12:00. You train for two hours, 12:00–2:00 p.m. You have to let your body recover, so you eat and recover. You get back out, you start training at 6:00 p.m. You train from 6:00–8:00, and now you go home, you shower, you eat dinner, you go to bed, you wake up, you do it again, right? **Those are two sessions.** Now imagine you get up at 3:00 a.m., and you train at 4:00 a.m. You go from 4:00–6:00, come home, eat breakfast, relax, etc. Now you're back at it again, 9:00–11:00 a.m. You relax, and now you're back at it again from 2:00–4:00 p.m. Then you're back at it again from 7:00–9:00 p.m. Look at how much more training I have done by simply starting at 4:00 a.m., right? So now you do that, and as the years go on, the separation that you have with your competitors and your peers just grows larger, and larger, and larger, and larger. And by year five or six, it doesn't matter what kind of work they do in the summer. They're never going to catch up because they're five years behind. If I start earlier, I can train more hours, and I know the other guys aren't doing it because I know what their training schedule is. So I know if I do this consistently over time, the gap is just gonna widen, and widen, and widen, and widen, and widen, and they won't be able to get that back. So to me, it was just common sense. I'm thinking: "How can I get an advantage? Start earlier. Yeah, let's do that!"

After this obsessive statement, he was then asked by the interviewer, "How do you develop that or where do you learn that from?"

Kobe responded:

"It's just a matter of what's important to you. **What's important to you?** For whatever reason . . . I didn't feel good about myself if I wasn't doing everything I could to be the best version of myself. If I felt I've left anything on the table, it would eat away at me. I wouldn't be able to look at myself in the mirror, and so the reason why I can retire now and be completely comfortable about it is because I know that I've done everything I could to be the basketball player I can be."

Kobe Bryant is the model of crushing the morning and winning the Fight Against Mediocrity. DOES THAT GET YOU PUMPED UP AND PISSED OFF FOR GREATNESS?! #POFG You shouldn't question why Kobe Bryant accomplished what he did during and after his basketball career. He truly separated himself from his peers, and you can do the same. It is simple math, and it is failure-proof.

## SOLITUDE

The early hours of the morning can be described as solitude. Merriam-Webster defines *solitude* as "the quality or state of being alone or remote from society." Solitude is where deep work and improvement can thrive, like a tender plant in a greenhouse that grows in the presence of moisture and nutrients. Solitude does not mean you are bored or lonely. In fact, studies show that solitude expands creativity and productivity. Researchers Christopher Long and James Averill say, "The paradigm experience of solitude is a state characterized by disengagement from the immediate demands of other people—a state of reduced social inhibition and increased freedom to select one's mental and physical activities." In an article written by Scott Barry Kaufman and Carolyn Gregoire in the Harvard Business Review they affirm, "it is often in solitary reflection that ideas are crystallized and insights formed."

Many of the world's greatest thinkers have given us examples of solitude. In Luke 5:16 (KJV) it teaches that Jesus Christ "withdrew himself into the wilderness, and prayed." J. K. Rowling secretly moved to a hotel, The Balmoral, in August 2006 for six months to find solitude and finish writing *Harry Potter and the Deathly Hollows*. Prolonged, focused solitude is like a stream that slowly wears down a stone over time. The constant and consistent pressure upon your goals in the early morning, like a stream, can provide the best way to solve difficult problems, learn more about yourself, and finish projects you've been putting off for years. Bill Gates is known for taking two "think weeks" per year. He spends seven days of solitude in a cabin in the middle of the forest. According to Business Insider Gates earns approximately $1,300 per second. At this rate, a week of his time has a cost of $786,240,000. I believe the earnings per second is based on his increased net worth over the course of 2021 so it may be exaggerated, but you get the point. Solitude is worth every penny.

Society preaches that being busy, running from meeting to meeting, signing documents on the go, and multi-tasking while on a zoom meeting is productive. Here's the truth: The human mind is a horrible multitasker. Multitasking is actually a false term: The mind is just bouncing from one idea to the next very quickly. Deep work will occur and difficult problems will be solved more efficiently by working in an environment of solitude. The early hours of the morning before 7:30 are the best time for solitude.

Once 7:30 a.m. rolls around, you are immediately enlisted in an ongoing war for your attention. The inevitable "urgent and important" tasks will hit you like a defensive lineman sacking a quarterback. From coworkers, children, friends, family, emails, texts, social media notifications, and the news, all with their own constant upheavals, to the neighbor who needs help moving a piano, and the second cousin twice removed who needs help recording his music video— everyone and everything is **pleading for your attention**. The greatest benefit of waking up early is you will avoid being on anyone else's agenda, and you can focus on YOU!

In many cases, your attention is monetized, which is why it is so difficult to find solitude. These platforms will only succeed into the next quarter if they show investors and advertisers that they can capture your attention long enough to make it worth the advertising dollars. It's not impossible to find solitude after 7:30 a.m., but it is extremely difficult. Just yesterday, two people told me they were unable to accomplish a planned goal during the day because "something came up." Neither were awake early enough to accomplish their most important tasks.

I know a few people who prefer to find solitude at night. That's great. Everyone has their own preferences. However, one of the reasons the early hours of the morning are a much better time for solitude than during the darkness of dusk is because the mind is rested and rejuvenated in the morning. Each morning, your willpower tank is at 100%. Every decision you make during the day slowly depletes your tank. That's why it's harder to resist sugary snacks late at night. You can achieve your best work in the morning because your willpower tank is at 100%. During the dead of night, you will be groggy and red-eyed, and the will-power tank will be at or near 0%.

## COMPOUNDING

Whether you realize it or not, you already have a morning routine. You have a ritual, a path that is well worn and used. Your current routine is either moving you closer to your goals or further from them. John Maxwell prophetically proclaims, "You will never change your life until you change something you do daily." Seems simple enough, right? There are really only two types of morning rituals: reactive and proactive. The reactive morning ritual is what 95% of people have. They may or may not wake up when the first alarm rings. They just do whatever life throws at them; there is no structure. This typically includes checking their phone before their feet even touch the floor. It is very similar to a tumbleweed in a windstorm. Most people are like tumbleweed: they go with the flow, moving whichever direction the wind blows, and the winds of life blow them wherever it pleases.

In a study done by Duke University, they discovered that 40% of the actions you take every day don't require a decision. They are habits you have formed. Nearly half of what you do every day is a habit. Where are your habits taking you? What are your habits? To find out, the first step is to track your daily actions to see where you spend your time. Doing this will make you aware and probably afraid of where you spend your precious minutes. Until you find out where you spend your time, the mind will convince you that you are more productive than you actually are. Your smartphone has the capability of tracking how much time you spend on each app. This can be used as an eye-opening exercise to see where you can cut time to spend on more productive tasks.

There is no one-size-fits-all morning routine. That's the beauty of life: you get to create your own path and pave your own future! The objective is to take advantage of the morning to make progress toward your life goals. Like I said, the morning is a God-given gift to the high achiever. Do the math: If you wake up early and give yourself one additional hour to work on you, that is an additional 365 hours every year. That is the equivalent of adding an additional 15.2 days or just over nine work weeks to your year. THAT IS INSANE! That's crazy talk. Now imagine if you create an additional two hours in the morning, double those numbers to 30.4 days (ONE MONTH!), or eighteen additional workweeks. Now let's compound that number over five years: If you give yourself an additional two hours every morning, that would compound into 152 additional days. Are you starting to see the separation created when you take advantage of the morning? There is no magic pill. However, there is the magic of the morning. Whatever you do or don't do in the morning will compound. Like Darren Hardy says, "The compound effect is always working. Either you make it work for you or it will have negative effects." I wrote this entire book between the hours of 4:00 a.m. and 7:00 a.m. What will you leave as your morning legacy?

## HEALTH

I'm sneaking health into this chapter because there are so many positive things to be said about exercising in the morning. I'm guessing that, if you are reading this book, you are aware of and working toward improving your health. If you aren't, I'd like to plead with you to repent and change.

Recall our discussion about Larry H. Miller in chapter 3: here is another lesson I learned from reading his autobiography. Larry H. Miller is an inspiration and surely was enlisted in The Fight Against Mediocrity. He and his organization have been and continue to be extremely generous to the communities they serve. Larry passed away in early 2009 at the age of 64 due to complications with type 2 diabetes, leaving behind a billion-dollar organization and a legacy of service.

Larry was relentless and passionate. At one point, after undertaking a new project, he essentially told his wife he would be gone for three years. There were some days he would skip breakfast and only carry with him a candy bar in the trunk of his car. Upon returning after a long day, the candy bar would still be there. Larry frequently ignored his health due to the work he was continually undertaking, whether it was acquiring a new dealership or putting the financing together to buy the Utah Jazz. Larry is an excellent example of hard work; you won't find many people in the world who work as hard as he did. I am, however, disappointed in his decisions to ignore his health, and he eventually paid the price. This is just one example, but there are millions of others around the world.

In an interview with KSL.com, Larry's sons, Brian and Steve, candidly shared their thoughts about their father's passing. Larry hid his health issues. It wasn't until the end when his rapid decline left him no recourse for recovery did they really know the full extent of his health problems. Brian said:

> "I'll look at my dad and see what work he did and the sacrifices he made . . . obviously there's a lot of good there. Couldn't he have done all that and made a few small choices to have been healthy and to still be with us doing those things?"

I can't help but think of how many more lives Larry could have impacted if he had taken care of his health.

There is a price to pay for choosing to live an unhealthy life. You can delay payments and ignore the daily duties of procuring a healthy lifestyle, but you're eventually required to pay a lump sum, and it is often in the form of an early departure from planet Earth. I urge and plead with you to take your health seriously. I see too many people assume they know how to live a healthy lifestyle but make costly mistakes because of their ignorance. Invest in your health, pay for a trainer or a nutrition expert, and exercise daily. Only listen to experts who have what you want. It sounds obvious, but don't hire an unhealthy trainer to help you get in shape . . . it really doesn't work that way.

This section is a bit somber, but that's how it felt for me when this principle hit home. I am and always have been an active individual, from basketball and professional unicycling to lifting daily at the gym. It wasn't until I was twenty-one that I finally understood the importance of nutrition and started studying the fuel my body needs and craves. Up until that point, I just ate whatever was placed in front of me. I read a book that taught me about the importance of protein, complex carbohydrates, and green vegetables. That newfound knowledge helped me change my beliefs and my behaviors. I started eating foods that helped me feel better. I realized that, much like a car needs clean oil and gas, my body needs the proper nutrients to function properly. I believe in eating foods that are God-made and not man-made. I am still learning and will never stop learning about my body and how the foods I ingest affect me and my future.

When I first started going to the gym religiously, my goal was to impress others with muscles and six-pack abs. That was my *why*. Not a bad starting point, and it was enough to motivate me at the time. As time went on, my *why* has shifted to the desire to run and play with my grandkids when I'm in my nineties. I don't want to lose valuable time with my loved ones and the opportunity to leave a legacy on the world because I didn't invest in my health.

You don't always see how your immediate action or inaction affects the future. As Darren Hardy says, "If you picked up that Big Mac and immediately fell to the ground clutching your chest from a heart attack, you might not go back for that second bite." We constantly trade short-term satisfaction for long-term dissatisfaction. Regarding health, begin with the end in mind.

The Bible teaches that our bodies are temples. Most likely, when you think of a temple, the following words come to mind: clean, pure, sacred, holy, sanctuary, inspiration, desirable, peaceful, and purposeful. Do those words correlate with how you are currently treating your body and health? In the New Testament, the very popular set of verses in 1 Corinthians 3:16-17 (KJV) read:

> Know ye not that ye are the
> temple of God, and that the Spirit
> of God dwelleth in you?
> If any man defile the temple of
> God, him shall God destroy; for

the temple of God is holy, which

temple ye are.

As you come to view your health and body as a temple, you will experience a paradigm shift. Drugs, alcohol, cigarettes, etc. have no place in or near a temple. They don't go hand in hand. Even if you don't believe in religion, the metaphor regarding your body's holy status is life changing. Temples are well manicured and cleaned frequently, which allows for temples to be a place of peace, serenity, and inspiration for worshipers. Do you feel peaceful when you eat a double cheeseburger, large fry, and chocolate shake? Or do you feel tired, sluggish, and slow? What you eat and do with your body affects the temple that houses your heart, mind, and soul. You need your heart, mind, and soul to be at 100% to accomplish your goals. Your body craves water, protein, complex carbohydrates, fruits, and vegetables. Not providing your body with these nutrients would be like buying a Ferrari and, instead of filling the tank with gas, you fill it full of sand.

Along with nutrition, exercise and stretching are required for a long, healthy life. I subscribe to what I recently referred to in Chapter 3 as The Sweat Rule. If you don't sweat, it doesn't work. I hear too many people complain that they aren't physically where they want to be. They typically either do not understand the nutrition behind getting results or they don't put in the effort required. If you aren't getting the results you want, lean in and push harder. Read everything you can about the foods that will help you reach your goal. Don't make excuses. Make sweat.

I'll ask you point-blank: Do you want to pay the price of health now or later? Everyone pays the price. Some will pay it over time by making time each day to exercise and eat a balanced diet. Others will choose to delay payments and have the debt called early. Do you want to make an impact on the world for as many minutes as you can? Make a conscious decision today which payment you will make.

## MY MORNING JOURNEY

During my teenage years, I was like a bear coming out of hibernation when I woke up in the morning. My siblings would play rock paper scissors for who would need to wake me up. I was notorious for getting out of bed just in the nick of time and sprinting like Usain Bolt to get ready for the day. My entire day was reactive as I rushed to catch up with the needs of the day. When I was nineteen, I left to serve a two-year service mission for the Church of Jesus Christ of Latter-Day Saints in the Yucatan Peninsula as I mentioned previously. During this two-year period, I followed a very strict schedule. We were required to wake up at 6:30 a.m. every day. For me, this seemed extremely early, and I was very nervous I couldn't maintain the schedule. However, I began to love the consistency of the morning routine and the structure it provided me. I felt confident as I took on the challenges of the day. For the first time in my life, I started to believe in my ability to wake up early.

After returning home, I slipped back into old habits. My desire and intentions to arise early were always strong and at the forefront of my mind. However, I wouldn't go to bed early enough and I'd hit the snooze button about a billion times. I was failing, and I was frustrated.

Around this time, I started exercising at 6:00 a.m. with my good friend, Sterling. It was a struggle for me to wake up. At one point, he drove to my home and came into my room to wake me as my alarm blasted right next to my ear. It was extremely discouraging, and I struggled to discipline myself to go to bed early. Each morning was a repeated failure. It felt like I was in the movie *Groundhog Day*.

There were, however, a few silver linings during this time. I would always add a few 7:30 a.m. classes to my school schedule to force myself to wake up early. I found that, if I had a responsibility, I was more likely to wake up. However, my willpower never seemed strong enough to roll me from the comfort of my bed. I didn't feel like I would ever conquer the morning. I felt like giving up.

It wasn't until I had struggled through a few tough situations that I started to become sick and tired of being sick and tired. I was engaged to be married, and because of my own uneasiness, I broke off the engagement. It was a bleak time for me. I decided it was time to make some critical changes. Things that had previously been should-dos, like waking up early, became must-dos. My standards increased, and I became pissed off for greatness #POFG. I started planning my weekly and daily routines with extreme consistency. I moved out of my parents' house. I became 100% responsible for myself and my time. I started going to bed early, and for the first time in my life, I started to say "no" when friends asked me to hang out. I realized that I had to set priorities and I couldn't just go with the flow or the crowd. I spent 1.5 hours on self-development in the morning. I was working on *me,* and it was long overdue!

As I started to see the results of my work, I became more motivated and felt momentum (Big Mo) working in my favor. Momentum is often referred to as "Big Mo." Big Mo occurs when good habits are performed consistently over time. It's like rolling a big rock down a mountain. At first, the rock can become lodged in a tight spot, making it difficult to move, but after a few strong attempts, it is dislodged and starts slowly rolling down the hill. As it picks up speed, it becomes impossible to stop, crushing anything in its path. The same occurs when you consistently perform good actions. The first few weeks feel like you are quite literally dislodging a large rock; it seems impossible. But after a few weeks, the rock slowly starts moving.

As time went on, my self-development in the morning increased until my days were filled with a constant downpour of audiobooks and YouTube motivational videos. I would listen to motivational videos all day. I started writing pages and pages of notes. I felt like I had just struck gold, and I was obsessed with my treasure. I continually asked myself why I had never learned these things before. Why didn't they teach them in school? Why doesn't everyone know these truths? Why doesn't everyone believe in accomplishing the impossible? I wrote quotes on sticky notes and placed them on the back of my phone, so I had a constant reminder of my new life. When they would get dirty and fall off, I started using clear packing tape to place them on the back of my phone. I'd read them over and over again. The fire in my belly was in full blaze and wouldn't be quenched anytime soon.

Every day, I became more and more dissatisfied with where I was in my life. My standards kept growing, and I sought ways I could improve my situation in all aspects of my life. I started eating extremely healthy and reached 8% body fat. As mentioned in the introduction, I competed in two triathlons and performed the biking portion on a 36-inch unicycle, which had been a goal I set for myself three years prior. It felt like everything I'd desired in my life but never made a priority were finally happening.

That same fire is still burning strong. I am more #PissedOffForGreatness than I ever have been. I am a member of the crazy ones that Steve Jobs said will change the world. I hope you noticed that I mentioned that I "raised my standards" several times. You don't get what you want in life; you get what you *must have* in life. You must raise your standards, and they must become non-negotiable. I found my "why" over time. I realized that I felt the same as Kobe when he said: "I didn't feel good about myself if I wasn't doing everything I could to be the best version of myself. If I felt I'd left anything on the table, it would eat away at me. I wouldn't be able to look at myself in the mirror. . ."

I hate, and I mean *hate*, the feeling of mediocrity. It makes me uneasy, tense, and frustrated. I've had the recurring realization that this life is my one shot to make a difference, and I'm not going to waste it.

I now wake up every day between 4:00 and 5:00 a.m. From where I was a short time ago, this is nothing short of a miracle. If I can do it, you can too. If you'd like to learn more about the step-by-step process I use to wake up early, visit www.thefightagainstmediocrity.com/morning.

Need motivation and more help? Scan the QR code to access free resources including my favorite motivational videos.

**CHAPTER FOUR - CRUSH THE MORNING**

# TAKE ACTION
## NOTHING CHANGES UNLESS SOMETHING CHANGES

- **Create a morning routine** that advances your self improvement and follow it religiously.
  - Visit www.TheFightAgainstMediocrity.com/Morning for help.
- **Make health a priority** by doing one or all of the following:
  - Hire a fitness or nutrition coach.
  - Follow a workout plan.
  - Use The Sweat Rule.
  - Plan and prepare your meals in advance.
- Find your "why" for living a healthy lifestyle.
- Remove addictive substances from your life.
- Spend time pondering what it means for your body to be a **temple that houses your heart, mind, and soul.**

# FREE ADDITIONAL RESOURCES

SCAN ME

or visit TheFightAgainstMediocrity.com/Resources to download an editable PDF of the action items.

# CHAPTER 5

## INVEST IN YOURSELF

**"You are your greatest asset. Put your time, effort and money into training, grooming, and encouraging your greatest asset." —Tom Hopkins**

One of the lies that the media bombards you with is that you can have it all for three easy payments of $39.95. I have a *big* problem with the "get rich quick" mentality. Anything that happens too quickly doesn't endure without a firm foundation.

The first step in building a home is digging a hole and laying the foundation. This analogy relates to investing in your mind and building your potential. The foundation of your life is who you are to your core. If everything else crumbles, your foundation is left standing among the debris. I see people who try to build incredible twenty-thousand-square-foot Beverly Hills mega-mansions on a foundation the size of a tiny home.

You can see how that will end, right? It won't last. The foundation isn't strong enough to hold the palace in place. This is akin to wanting to achieve great success without building your foundation to the appropriate size. If you have mansion-sized ambitions, you have to build a mansion-sized foundation.

The best investments you will ever make are in the six inches between your ears. If you're going to go broke, go broke investing in yourself. The more you know, the more you can grow. Building a Beverly Hills–sized foundation takes time and requires a set of well-engineered plans to ensure long-term stability. Building a foundation of success for your life will take time and can seem slow and tedious, but once the walls go up, it is paramount that your foundation is the right size: it will make or break your future growth and potential.

## LEARN TO EARN $

In precisely the same way your body is made up of all the nutrients you digest, your mind is the sum of everything you see, hear, and experience. Elbert Hubbard said, "The recipe for perpetual ignorance is: Be satisfied with your opinions and content with your knowledge."

The average American reads, hold on, give me a moment to count. . . just one book per year! The average CEO reads four to five books a month, and it is rumored that people like Teddy Roosevelt would often read two books a day. Harvey Mackay from *The Business Journals* said that "business people who read at least seven business books a year earn over **2.3 times** more than those who read only one per year." Want a quick pay raise? Start reading! According to research from Thomas Crowley, 85% of self-made millionaires read two or more books per month. Unfortunately, I'm not talking about Harry Potter. The books that will help you the most are centered on self-development, business, relationships, and topics within your industry. It is also a good habit to read books outside your industry or interests to get different perspectives. Dr. Suess once said, "The more you read, the more things you will know. The more that you learn, the more places you'll go." I have experienced the enormous benefits of reading in my life. It has not only allowed me to build more wealth, but it has also made me a better husband and friend. I want to make this extremely clear: If you complain about your current situation in life, but you spend your nights, weekends, and free time doing things other than reading and learning, your circumstances will never change.

Reading books is just one of the many tools available to improve your situation. The first investment I made that was more than the price of a book provided a return of 20X in just one week. I invested $99 and made over $2,000 in return in only seven days. I know what you are thinking, and no, I did not join a pyramid scheme or sell my organs. My first full-time sales position was for a startup tech company in Silicon Slopes. I was making the jump from a stable nine-to-five accounting job to a 100% commission sales position. Despite my fears and trepidations, I was 100% invested and believed that, with hard work, I would succeed. I invested in a sales and self-development program that cost $99. I was the only one in the office who was willing to invest the money. We were starting off. Sales were picking up slowly, but $99 was a steep price for most of us. I put my head down and listened to the program every spare minute I had. I would listen, make cold calls, and then listen some more. Within a few days of listening and implementing what I was learning, I had learned sales psychology and techniques that shifted my paradigms significantly. I made a sale, then another, then one more for good measure. In just seven days, I earned three sales from the principles I applied and brought home a nice $2,000 commission check. Needless to say, after seeing my results, everyone in the office made the same investment. The key lesson is, never hesitate to invest in yourself. Don't second-guess it. You will be presented with grand opportunities in the future, but if you don't invest time and money into yourself, you won't be prepared to seize them. Always look for opportunities to invest in the six inches between your ears.

## THE 3 PERCENT RULE

In Chapter 3, life was compared to a moving river: You are either swimming upstream against the running water or slowly drifting downstream. Learning has a direct correlation with the upstream or downstream motions in your life. If you stop learning, how can you expect to lead yourself, your family, and your team upstream?

Brian Tracy is known for the *3 percent rule*. He says that whatever your current income is, take 3% and invest it back into yourself. Invest it in an Audible account, books, online universities, industry conferences, etc. Choosing to invest money in yourself is the most important investment you will ever make. The real treasure is that, once you've invested in yourself, your investment can't be taken from you. The knowledge and skills you obtain by investing time and money into yourself cannot be taxed or taken away from you. I invite you to start using the 3 percent rule in your life as the minimum investment you make in yourself. If you want faster results, I challenge you to invest 5-10% of your income back into yourself.

## KNOWLEDGE IS NOT POWER

There is a reason this book is titled *Talk Is Cheap*. After you've invested a minimum of 3% into yourself, you are still missing an important ingredient of success: **ACTION!** Darren

Hardy prophetically said, "Knowledge is not power. That's a myth. It is the potential for power, but it is not power itself. It's not what you learn or what you know; **it's what you do with what you know and learn.**"

Many success seekers overlook not only making time to learn, but creating a plan to implement what they've learned. Make your plan for implementation a priority after each book you read, program you complete, or conference you attend. For example, if you attend a conference on Thursday, plan adequate time on Friday to apply what you've learned. Otherwise, the time spent learning will be for naught.

Research has shown that, within one hour of learning a new idea, you will already have forgotten about 50% of the information. That's bad, but it gets worse. After just twenty-four hours, you will have forgotten 70%, on average, and after one week of information slowly draining from your brain, all that remains is about 10%. If you wait one week to make an implementation plan, you have already forgotten 90% of what you learned. That is an extremely disturbing piece of information. If, after one week, you haven't made plans to apply what you learned, then you wasted your time and money, plain and simple.

Don't blame your brain; it is just doing its job. The brain is very efficient and does not need to remember trivial information. For example, I was recently at the airport, and I needed to remember where I parked my car upon arrival, but now that I'm home, I don't want my brain to remember Row G. The brain forgets information, so you don't experience information overload. So, if the goal is long-term behavior change (it is!) then what you do immediately after learning will make or break your progression.

Let's compare learning to walking through a field of tall grass. If you've ever done it, you'll know that, after you've walked through the field, you can see where you traveled from the flattened grass. If you go back the next day, the grass will have straightened, and there will be no distinguishable path. On the other hand, if you walk the same path multiple times a day for a few months, eventually you will wear a permanent path in the field. Learning is very similar: it takes repetition to truly learn and apply something to your life.

There are ways to signal to the brain that a piece of information is important to boost retention. One of the best ways is to recall information from memory. When the brain is asked to recall information, the path in the brain becomes easier to travel, like walking in a field of long grass. The more times someone travels the same path, the easier it is to identify. It works for everything, not just information. For example, watch Steph Curry shoot a basketball versus someone else for the first time. Steph's path is worn so deep that it is just dirt. His brain knows what to do and where to go because he has recalled the information so many times. On the other hand, a first-time basketball player looks like he is wading through the grass with a machete, like the brain has no idea where to go. Repeated practice and recall are the keys to making lasting change reality. Reading a book just one time is unlikely to have a huge impact on your life, but if you read it several times, share what you learned with a friend, put a set of flashcards near your desk for review, and apply something you learned daily, you will create a permanent path that will change your life.

You can learn more about information retention from the book *Make It Stick* by Peter C. Brown, Henry L. Roediger III, and Mark A. McDaniel. In the book, they teach about the importance of recalling information. According to the authors, recall does not mean reread. Rereading your notes is like jumping over a field of grass: no path is created. Cramming for a test the night before and dumping all the information onto the paper just to forget it as you walk out of class is completely useless. Instead, immediately after a training session, take a blank sheet of paper and write down everything you remember from memory. Do it again and again for the days and weeks following, and you will be well on your way to permanent retention and mastery. A study done by Dr. Henry Roediger showed that recalling information by memory in the hours and days after learning can increase retention by nearly two times!

Here is a list of ideas to help you retain information and make a lasting change:

- Schedule time to recall information immediately after training and in the following days.
- Use flashcards to review information.
- As a leader, plan follow-up time to allow your team time to recall information.
- Teach what you learned to someone else.
- Set a time and place on your calendar to act on what you've learned.

None of the ideas above are sexy, and they all require conscious effort, but they provide real results on your path to making lasting change. As my mentor, Jeff Shore, frequently says, "The destination called mastery is on a road called repetition."

## FIND A MENTOR

While studying for my undergraduate degree, I was frequently told to find a mentor. This concept always felt extremely daunting because I'd assumed I needed to convince a billionaire in an ivory tower to teach me about success. I wondered how anyone could get a mentor like that. They are probably extremely busy. Why would they want to spend time with someone like me? Because of that twisted paradigm, I quickly dismissed the idea of getting a mentor. Then I heard a new definition of "mentor": A mentor is someone who has what you want or is the type of person you want to become. You could follow a mentor without ever meeting them. Let me explain: because of how easily information is shared on the internet, more and more individuals can share the knowledge they have gained via books, videos, podcasts, webinars, social media posts, virtual conferences, online universities, etc. This information paradise makes it easier than ever to learn from the best in the world. **This is the key: pick one or two people who have what you want or are the people you want to become and follow them obsessively.** Read and listen to all their content, then read and listen to it again and again! It is so important to narrow it down to just one or two people; otherwise, you won't be able to focus enough to have the information change you. Darren Hardy taught me that instead of reading thirty books one time, it is far more beneficial to read one book thirty times. The same thing applies to mentors. Less is more. Be selective with who you follow. Check their integrity: you become who you are surrounded by.

## A $200,000 MISTAKE

What you don't know *can* hurt you. My father has always been very entrepreneurial. He started and sold a few small businesses in the first years of my parents' marriage. He is the stereotypical entrepreneur who went to college but dropped out because he couldn't afford it and didn't enjoy it. From a young age, he was responsible for purchasing his clothes, school supplies, and sports equipment. In third grade, he worked at a local dairy after school and during the summers. He grew up working in construction framing and painting. During the early years of my parents' marriage, my dad worked on his business during the day and painted houses at night to make ends meet. I've never once heard him complain about the hard times he's gone through. He is truly grateful for the experiences that made him who he is.

One of his most influential business leadership experiences occurred when he started a home-building company with the help of his father-in-law in 1996, just three years after I was born. Like I mentioned before, my dad lived and breathed hard work, but no one taught him how to run a home-building company. As a result of his lack of industry knowledge, he lost $200,000 in the first two years of business. Yikes! I can't even imagine how that conversation went when he drove to my grandpa's house to tell him the news. If you think asking for someone's hand in marriage is hard, imagine asking for forgiveness for losing $200,000! My father knew something needed to change, so he started attending industry conferences and joined a home-builders group where consultants taught industry standards. He went on to build one of the largest home-building companies in Utah and Idaho.

The most important takeaway from this lesson is, don't let the unknown keep you from starting. Although my dad lost enough money to buy a Rolls Royce, he didn't let what he didn't know keep him from starting. There likely wasn't a way for him to avoid many of the pains he experienced in the early days of his business, but they made him successful today. Don't be afraid to make mistakes; be afraid of not learning the lessons mistakes teach.

Whatever business you are in, become an expert. My dad frequently says that industry conferences are what has made him successful in the home-building industry. He is never afraid to spend money on education: it can be the difference between making or losing money. The most successful people in the world are masters of their crafts.

## COLLEGE

There isn't a one-size-fits-all approach to education. For some people, college may be the perfect fit, while for others, it is a terrible option. Too many parents and teachers push one option, as if it is the only path to take. Nothing could be further from the truth. Going to college doesn't make someone smart or successful: It's what you *do* that makes the difference. There are a growing number of college alternatives, including technical and trade schools. You can often get paid while attending school and learn a valuable trade skill at the same time. Companies like Google and Tesla have even said that they no longer require applicants to have a college degree.

For some, college and technical schools may be out of the question altogether. If this describes you, dive into your work and give it 100%. I promise that, as you become an expert in your field, you will be duly compensated.

I studied accounting for my undergraduate degree. It seemed like a great way to learn the language of business and a great springboard for my ultimate goal of starting a business. I'll share three things that drove me absolutely nuts about my undergraduate experience.

The first was the most-asked question by my peers:, "Will this be on the test?" WHAT? We are preparing to run finances for businesses, and everyone was simply worried if it would be on the test! Screw the test! Teach me how to manage the numbers for a business; teach me how to run QuickBooks; teach me skills I can use tomorrow to get a job or start a business.

The second was the ultimate goal of the accounting program: to herd as many of the accounting students as possible into the largest accounting firms in the state of Utah. If the school could place more students at these firms, it would look better to prospective students. What about other career paths? I could do just about anything in business with an accounting degree, right? Nope. According to the university, just the large accounting firms. That's all we were encouraged to pursue.

Lastly, as an undergraduate in accounting with nearly four years and over 120 credit-hours under my belt, I only took six classes (18 credit-hours) that other business students did not to graduate with a degree in accounting. How does that make any sense? That equates to roughly one semester of classes dedicated to accounting! In my opinion, it should be the other way around. I should only take six classes that *did not* have to do with accounting.

I'll step off my soapbox, but I hope you see the point. Just because you have a college degree, it doesn't mean you are an expert. If you choose to go to college, make sure you fill your time with part-time jobs, extracurricular activities, and networking.

If you choose an alternative to college, don't feel bad for going against the norm. Over time, this stereotype will change as colleges become overpriced and provide less and less real-world value.

I have received criticism for my opinion about college. Many people have told me that, without college, we wouldn't have doctors, engineers, and dentists. These people are confusing college with education. College is not the only way to learn a skill. I predict there will be more and more career-specific education options in the future. Instead of going to college for four years to only take six accounting classes, I would have preferred one or two years of school with 18 accounting classes.

## SO GOOD THEY CAN'T IGNORE YOU

For many of you, college is years in the past, or maybe college wasn't even in the cards. Regardless of your current situation, there is a way for you to have increased autonomy, compensation, and fulfillment. In Cal Newport's book *So Good They Can't Ignore You*, he outlines the rules for becoming an expert in any field. The title of the book comes from a quote by Steve Martin who is frequently asked by aspiring comedians how to make it in show business. His response isn't what they want to hear: be "so good they can't ignore you." In essence, he encourages them to practice, fail, get up, try again, and then repeat that process until they get results.

Malcolm Gladwell's rule for becoming a true expert, from his book, *Outliers*, is ten thousand hours of practice. It takes deliberate, dedicated practice to become an expert.

Deliberate practice is very different from going through the motions. It requires practice and effort outside of your comfort zone and normal business hours. It is going above and beyond what your peers' thought possible. Many of them may make fun of you for being too "obsessed" or working too hard. That's simply the mark of an achiever.

I think too often we assume that, if we aren't passionate about something, we shouldn't pursue it. I've found that passion follows expertise. As you become better, you will become more passionate. Everyone sucks at first. Everyone starts with zero followers.

## BE CURIOUS

The most successful people in the world are extremely curious. They never stop asking questions, never assuming they know the entire story. The moment you assume you know everything, that is moment you stop growing and start declining.

Sam Walton, founder of Wal-Mart, was known for always carrying around a yellow notepad and constantly asking questions. He was widely known for visiting the stores of competitors, questioning everything they did, then copying the best ideas. There is little question about his recipe for success: He was constantly learning and improving. That is the simple success formula.

Albert Einstein once said, "I have no special talent. I am only passionately curious." Here are some ideas you can use to be more curious:

- Ask questions and listen: seek to understand then to be understood.
- Carry a notepad to write notes and ideas.
- Try something new.
- Call someone in your field and pick their brain to find out how they do things.
- Once again, ASK QUESTIONS. This is the most underused method of curiosity. I see too many people who are afraid to ask questions because they don't want to look stupid. In my opinion, it is stupid not to ask questions. Most of the time everyone around you has the same question but is too afraid to ask. ASK QUESTIONS!

Curiosity is a habit that is built over time as you continually seek to become better. Never take things at face value. Always seek to learn, and remember what Einstein said: "I have no special talent. I am only passionately curious."

## NEVER STOP LEARNING

The moment you think you know it all, think again. The relentless and life-long pursuit of learning is required in The Fight Against Mediocrity. There is always something to learn and always a way to improve. Successful people are coachable and eager to learn new ways of doing things. Be willing to change and pivot as you learn new ideas.

Blockbuster is a great example of what not to do. If you don't remember what Blockbuster is, you're not alone. They failed because they weren't willing to learn and change. It was a DVD rental brick-and-mortar store. When Netflix came along and started mailing DVDs and streaming online movies, they offered to sell to Blockbuster for $50 million. Blockbuster was worth $6 billion at the time. When Netflix founders met with Blockbuster CEO John Antioco in 2000 to discuss the purchase, they were quickly dismissed. One Netflix founder, Marc Randolph, said Antioco had to hold back laughter during the meeting. Fast-forward ten years, and Blockbuster was bankrupt. Blockbuster was "floating" on their previous success and assumed they were too big to fail. There are only two directions in life: upstream or downstream. When you aren't paddling upstream, innovating along the way, you are drifting downstream to your demise.

Jeff Bezos is famous for his Day One mentality. A Day One mentality means acting like a startup company. If you've ever worked for or founded a startup, you undoubtedly know that it is a rollercoaster. Each day brings a new obstacle or challenge, and each team member is required to wear essentially a million different hats. The small wins are celebrated with energy usually reserved for the Super Bowl while losses can seem like a mountain just crumbled on top of you. Even through the roller coaster ride, there is a "fire in the belly" type of feeling at a startup, a "do whatever it takes" mentality. Everyone on the team bands together to create something that has never been done before. At a startup, decisions are made quickly, and everyone is required to be nimble. Feedback from customers is discussed openly, and changes are implemented within hours. Startups have passion, something ivory tower corporate prestige often suffocates. Obviously, with 600,000 employees, Amazon is well beyond day one, but they still follow the same principle.

Always be curious, coachable, and eager to learn something new. Don't ever be afraid to ask questions and reach out to people who have what you want. In an all-hands meeting, Bezos was asked, "What does day two look like?" He responded, "Day two is stasis, followed by irrelevance, followed by an excruciating painful decline, followed by death. That is why it is always Day One." Now, maybe that mentality is a slippery slope fallacy, but the moral of the story remains the same: overcome complacency, because complacency leads to death—the death of potential and growth.

Need motivation and more help? Scan the QR code to access free resources including my favorite motivational videos.

**CHAPTER FIVE - INVEST IN YOURSELF**

# TAKE ACTION
## NOTHING CHANGES UNLESS SOMETHING CHANGES

- **Find a mentor** and absorb all the information you can from them (books, articles, podcasts, YouTube, etc.).
- **Write down and implement** your improvement ideas like Sam Walton.
- **Read more books!** Scan the QR code below for my recommendations.
- Start **investing a minimum of 3%** of your income into self-development right now!
- Write **"Day One Mentality"** on a sticky note and put it somewhere you'll see it every day.
- Schedule time to recall and implement what you learn.
- Regularly attend conferences and masterminds.

# FREE
# ADDITIONAL
# RESOURCES

SCAN ME

or visit TheFightAgainstMediocrity.com/Resources to download an editable PDF of the action items.

# CHAPTER 6

## DEADLINES

**"If you're doing the same things as everyone else, don't be surprised when you end up like everyone else. To be different, you have to do something different." —Kevin Kartchner**

Merriam-Webster defines a deadline as:

1. A line drawn within or around a prison that a prisoner passes at the risk of being shot

2. A date or time before which something must be done

3. The time after which copy is not accepted for a particular issue of a publication

In the late 1800s, the word *deadline* was primarily referred to a death line drawn on the ground at prisons: If prisoners chose to cross the line, they would be shot. Deadlines were a life-or-death situation. Just like past prison rules, if you fail to set and keep deadlines, your goals will be shot down by the demands and pressures of the world around you. Your goals and dreams are on the chopping block if you choose to ignore deadlines.

## CREATE DEADLINES

There are only two types of people in this world: people who complete homework at 11:58 p.m., one minute before it's due, and people who complete homework one minute after it is assigned to them. Until now, I have been the first person, but I'm getting better. I remember one night, during my undergraduate degree (or more appropriately, in the early morning around 2:00 or 3:00 a.m.), I was completing a project due later that day. In those early hours, I had a sudden realization of how important deadlines are to my success. Here I was grinding away at 2:00 a.m. for a class I didn't even enjoy, and I was doing it because of a **deadline**. A deadline had caused me to decide to stay up late, lose sleep, and finish a project. **A deadline.** Then it hit me like a Ford F-350: WHY DON'T I CREATE DEADLINES FOR THINGS I ACTUALLY WANT TO DO? If I was willing to stay up until 2:00 a.m. for some bogus class, why wasn't I willing to do the same for my dreams? Why was it so easy to turn down dinner with friends

112

and family when I had to go to class, but I quickly dismissed appointments with myself to work on my goals? It was so clear to me that I needed to set deadlines and appointments with myself and make the same type of commitment I had to finish the pointless project at 2:00 a.m.

This requires an abnormal amount of discipline, which is why it is so rare that people stick to self-imposed deadlines. Brian Tracy says only 2% of people can make and keep commitments to themselves. The rest require someone hovering over them to get things done. **I'll let you in on a secret. If there is no deadline or it is not on your calendar, it is very unlikely it will ever happen.**

No deadline always results in defeat. No deadline leads to delusion and uncertainty. When you create a personal deadline, treat it as such and tell others you are busy. It is crucial to have integrity, not only with others but also with yourself. If you tell yourself you are going to do something, do it! Otherwise, you lose confidence in yourself and your ability to keep your word.

## DEADLINES & DIAMONDS

There is truth in the statement, "When you wait until the last minute, it only takes a minute." Deadlines create pressure that typically results in increased productivity and speed. Think about how a sports team plays in the final two minutes of a tied Super Bowl versus a pickup game with no time limit or scoreboard: **When there is pressure, performance improves and increases.** A diamond is formed only after pressure forces coal to crystalize. Darren Hardy calls it a *Genesis deadline*: God set an example for us when He created heaven and earth in six days. We, too, must set unreasonable deadlines that push us to do the impossible. Deadlines provide increased clarity and focus which leads to greater achievement and increased productivity.

At the end of the day, if you don't make sacrifices for what you want, what you want will be sacrificed. Create a sense of urgency regarding your goals and dreams. Set Genesis deadlines when pursuing your goals. Get focused and say no to activities that don't take you closer to your goals.

## PARKINSON'S LAW & HORSTMAN'S COROLLARY

Parkinson's law states that work expands to fit the time allotted: The more time you allot for a project, the more time it will take you. Horstman's corollary is similar to Parkinson's law: work contracts to the time allotted. I experience this all the time when I go to the gym. When I exercise during lunch, I only have about 45 minutes, so I fit my workout into that time slot. However, if I go to the gym on a Saturday morning with no deadline, I could be there for two hours and complete the same workout that only took 45 minutes during lunch the day before. The workout will expand or contract to the amount of time I provide.

High achievers get more done in less time with *time blocking*. In very simple terms, time blocking eliminates multitasking and promotes intense focus over a short period of time. It's like cooking rice in an Instant Pot versus using a pot of boiling water: It takes half the time to get the same amount of work done. In Jeb Blount's book *Fanatical Prospecting*, he teaches salespeople to remove all distractions including Facebook, cat videos, social media, text messages, emails, etc., and focus a specific amount of time on a specific activity. Jeb teaches outbound prospecting and finds that, when time blocking, salespeople who typically make a whopping seven dials in two hours can make twenty-five calls and set two appointments in just thirty minutes. Focusing on one activity at a time instead of multitasking increases productivity by 30% or more! Imagine all you can do with 30% more productivity!

Silicon Slopes legend, Peter Thiel, frequently asks the question: "How can you achieve your ten-year plan in the next six months?" Understanding Parkinson's law and Horstman's corollary proves that, if you condense your timeframe and increase focus, you magically get more done in less time. Presto!

## YOU HAVE DEADLINES

No matter what your situation, you have deadlines every day. Even if you are jobless and homeless, you still have a deadline of finding food and water. Some of the most common deadlines are getting to the office in the morning, preparing a proposal for a client, picking up kids from sports, attending family activities, etc. The problem is that most people have reactive deadlines: The deadlines they are fulfilling are set for them by someone else, and they simply "react." Your life will change when you start making and keeping **proactive deadlines**. Proactive deadlines are set by you, for you. These are the hardest to keep and the easiest to brush off. They are typically deadlines for tasks that fall into quadrant two on the Time Management Matrix. Quadrant II is "Important and Not Urgent" as seen on the graphic below. I'll explain the other quadrants on the next page.

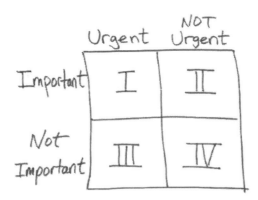

"Important and Not Urgent" tasks impact your life very little if missed for a few days or weeks. But, if they are missed for years and decades, well, let's just say you'll pay the price. A great example is health and exercise. If you don't exercise for a month, you probably won't notice a huge difference in your overall health, and you will probably follow the same routine with little difficulty. However, let's say you don't care for your body for thirty years. What happens? Look back to Chapter 4's illustration of Larry H. Miller. Other items that fall into quadrant II are reading, planning, preparing, spending time with friends and family, going on a date with your significant other, and personal development.

Here is a brief explanation of quadrants I, II, III, and IV.

- **Quadrant I** consists of tasks that are urgent and important. These are tasks that you didn't plan or prepare for but need to get done right away, like a phone call from an upset customer.
- **Quadrant II** is important and not urgent tasks, like eating healthily and exercising.
- **Quadrant III** consists of activities that are urgent and not important. Examples include email management and irrelevant meetings.

- Lastly, **quadrant IV** consists of not urgent and not important tasks. Examples include social media, watching TV, gossip, and spam email.

Spend as much time as possible in quadrant II, delegate quadrant III, reduce quadrant I, and completely remove items from quadrant IV. To learn more about the four quadrants, I highly recommend reading *Seven Habits of Highly Effective People* by Stephen Covey.

It requires vision, desire, belief, and sacrifice to make and keep personal deadlines. Very few people will ever try it, and even fewer will successfully achieve it. Engaging your emotions plays a huge role in achievement. If you set a deadline for yourself, like waking up early or reading a book, and you fail to keep said commitment, you should be disgusted with yourself. Don't wallow in self-pity, but be disgusted and horrified with yourself. Remind yourself to never let it happen again. You will never raise the quality of your life unless you raise your standards.

Having no deadlines in your life is like dropping yourself in the middle of the ocean in a rowboat with no paddle. You will just drift around, going nowhere. Imagine a world without deadlines. Picture for a moment if every student and teacher arrived at class whenever they wanted, the students turned in assignments when they felt like it, sports teams showed up to games during halftime, and there was no scoreboard to let us know that the game was tied with thirty seconds left. Deadlines create urgency! No deadline means no destination.

It drives me nuts when someone says, "Yeah, we should do that sometime." In my mind, I think, "Yo, my friend, sometime, means no time." If you want something to happen, set a date, time, and place and add it to your calendar.

## GOALS

Merriam-Webster defines a *goal* as "the end toward which effort is directed." **The only difference between a goal and a dream is a deadline.** Deadlines demand commitment and focus. They turn "someday" into "today." Goal achievement is nearly impossible until there is a deadline. If your deadline was "it happens when it happens," then I hope this chapter has helped you feel the urgency to change.

Along with having a deadline, write your goals down daily to reach them faster. When you write your goals daily, you increase the odds of achieving them by 42%, according to psychology professor Dr. Gail Matthews of the Dominican University of California. Writing them down daily forces you to clarify what you want. Leaving your goals in your brain causes ambiguity, but once they are on paper and have a deadline, you'll start to see them come to life. The goals you write down should scare you. There needs to be a big payoff and a big reason to push for the goals you set for yourself. If it doesn't inspire and motivate you, then it isn't big enough. Bill Gates wisely said, "Most people overestimate what they can do in one year and underestimate what they can accomplish in ten years."

It should be scary how badly you need to accomplish your goals. Other people should use the words *obsessed*, *relentless*, and even *annoying* to describe you. The most telling separation from average to top 1% is having an idea and acting on it immediately. Just commit, especially if you don't know how everything will play out!

In Sean Covey's book *The Four Disciplines of Execution*, he explains that effective goals need to be deeply embedded in our minds. That sounds pretty basic, right? He illustrates this by teaching with the following example: shake a deeply committed person awake at 2:00 a.m. and yell "What's the goal?" When they come to, they'll immediately respond by answering with the goal. Goals must be at the forefront of your mind at all times.

Without goals, there is no purpose or urgency. You are merely floating through life. As the seven-time Mr. Olympia, Arnold Schwarzenegger, said, "You can have the best boat or the best plane, but if you don't know where you are going, you will never get anywhere." Once you've made your goals and set deadlines, schedule checkpoints. What will happen in the next week, month, quarter, and year from today to arrive on time at your destination? Figure out the daily habits and rituals required to complete your goals and track them every single day. For example, if your goal is to have six-pack abs, set a daily habit to exercise for sixty minutes, six days per week. If you get to the end of the week and you've only exercised 2/6 times, you can easily see you are off course to hit your goal. Your daily actions are the steppingstones that help you inch toward your goal. They may seem small and insignificant, but after sixty days of consistent baby steps, you will be shocked at how far you've traveled. Execute your plan and re-evaluate weekly, monthly, quarterly, and yearly. It's easy to do, but because it is easy, most people give it very little attention.

## FLOSSING

I recently had a dentist appointment where they checked the health of my gums. I didn't even know that was a thing. Anyways, I didn't fail, but I didn't get an A+ either. The dental assistant told me that, if I didn't want to have issues in the future, I was going to need to start flossing. That's not the first time they've told me that. This time, I committed to flossing every single day. At first, it was like torture, which is funny because it only takes about sixty seconds to floss. Even after 45 days, I still found it took a conscious effort to floss. It wasn't until about 120 days of consistently flossing that it became a habit. My next appointment with the dentist was six months later, and when they called to remind me, I was so excited to see the results of my hard work. They told me I was the first person that was excited to get a reminder call about a dental appointment. The dental assistant measured my gums, and lo and behold, they were healthy, and I received an A+ rating. I told them I had flossed every single day, and to my amazement, they were surprised. They told me that very few people ever follow through on a dentist's advice to floss every day.

There are so many lessons in this story. The first is that consistency will beat a one-time effort 100% of the time. I did the floss math, and six months of flossing for sixty seconds per day adds up to three hours. Imagine for a moment that, instead of spacing it out over 180 days, I chose to floss for three hours right before my dentist appointment. Did you just taste blood? I would end up with a bloody mess instead of beautifully manicured gums.

**The easy thing to do is also the hardest thing to do.** Reread that last sentence one more time. It is *so easy* to floss sixty seconds every day, almost suspiciously easy. And that is why hardly anyone does it. It seems too easy to make a difference, but that's just it: the easy things make the biggest difference. It is easy to read a book, write down your goals, visualize who you want to be, etc. People tend to prefer the big, sexy, flashy things, not the simple tasks. The process required for success is rarely sexy. It's usually boring, consistent, and filled with mind-numbing actions repeated again and again. Success is like flossing every day. Don't let the simpleness of the task fool you.

Flossing is all it took to go from unhealthy to healthy gums. Similarly, there are typically only one or two things you need to do every day to reach your goal. Michael Phelps is one of the greatest examples of this phenomenon. Phelps is arguably the best swimmer of all time. He is truly world-class. To get there, he did one thing: he swam every day for six hours per day. No days off. Well, his coach did let him leave fifteen minutes early once to go to a school dance.

Pick what you want to be world-class at and find the one or two things you need to do every single day to get there. John Maxwell said he became an expert in leadership by studying leadership one hour a day for five years. Let good habits become your master. It isn't sexy, but the results will be.

In the Bible, in Isaiah chapter 28 (KJV), it says, "For precept must be upon precept, precept upon precept; line upon line, line upon line; here a little, and they're a little." If the progress seems slow at first, don't worry. That's how success happens. There is no such thing as an overnight success.

My wife, Lauren, started an online clothing boutique and was doing extremely well for the first few months but wondered why she wasn't selling more clothes. She was discouraged and worried that her customers didn't like her clothing. As I thought about her situation, it dawned on me that success can't happen quickly. Sure, there are exceptions to the rule, but nine out of ten times, it takes time. Let me explain. This is Lauren's first business, and she is going through the same learning process every entrepreneur experiences. If she opened her boutique, Klemont Clothing, and suddenly made millions of dollars with no business experience, everyone would do the same thing. It would be a cheap experience. That's not how it works. It has to be hard. It has to be slow at first. It takes time to learn the fundamentals. If success came easy, there would be no satisfaction in the journey to achievement.

Do the work every day, especially when you don't feel like it, and watch the magic of "flossing" change your life.

## INCREASE SALES USING DEADLINES

"HUGE SALE THIS WEEKEND ONLY!" This banner is strung across every retail store at some point during the year. Why do sales have deadlines? Why isn't every day Black Friday? Promotional deadlines drive *urgency* to the buyer. It is a paradox in many sales environments that, if you want to increase sales, just let the prospective buyers know that, come Monday morning, prices are increasing. The fear of missing out on a good deal creates a sense of urgency to make a purchase.

## KEEPING COMMITMENTS AND DEADLINES

We've covered deadlines extensively, but here is one more crucial concept when it comes to keeping the commitments and deadlines you make with yourself: It's no secret that New Year's resolutions are typically abandoned within the first few weeks of the year. Humans are driven by habits, and creating new habits is difficult. Most people default to old habits when things get hard.

Unfortunately, few people have the discipline required to keep the deadlines they set for themselves that push them toward their dreams and goals. This is typically because of the "someday" excuse. "Someday I'll start exercising, writing, reading, etc." Someday may never come. Today is the day to Fight Against Mediocrity and pursue your goals with a full head of steam. Only 2% of people have the discipline required to keep self-imposed deadlines. When I mentioned the "someday" excuse, did a goal come to mind? Act on it right now. Put this book down and act! **You might be scared to start, but you should be more scared of never starting.** Reread that.

## THE DARK SIDE OF DEADLINES

Despite the benefits deadlines can have in your life to push you to work harder and do more, they do have a dark side. Deadlines can cause humans to do extraordinary things, but they also cause many to do irrational things. It is crucial to remember that the majority of your deadlines are not life-threatening. Yes, there are consequences, but just because you miss a deadline doesn't mean the sun won't rise in the morning. A perfect example is getting married just because you have a set date, even though you feel unsure about the relationship. I've been there. It's really hard, but you must consider both the short- and long-term consequences. This is just one example of knowing when to ignore a deadline.

There is a difference between reactive deadlines (deadlines set for you by someone else) and proactive deadlines (deadlines set by yourself), as mentioned earlier in this chapter. Never let a reactive deadline make you do something that is going to be bad for your future. This can be especially true when you are making difficult or large life decisions. It depends on the situation, but you'd be surprised at how many deadlines can be made flexible. Don't put yourself in a bad business or life situation to meet a deadline. I know this seems very counterintuitive to everything in this chapter, but it actually ties together perfectly. Deadlines are a double-edged sword. Make sure you use them to your advantage.

Need motivation and more help? Scan the QR code to access free resources including my favorite motivational videos.

**CHAPTER SIX - DEADLINES**

# TAKE ACTION
## NOTHING CHANGES UNLESS SOMETHING CHANGES

- Use Google Calendar (or the calendar of your preference) and **schedule every deadline** you create. **Treat deadlines as sacred time commitments.**
- Answer the question: **"How can I achieve my ten-year plan in the next six months?"**
- **Floss every day**, a.k.a., find two to three activities that if done daily will take you closer to your goal.
- **Use time blocking** (30–90 minutes of uninterrupted, distraction-free periods of time) to get 30% more done in shorter amounts of time.

or visit TheFightAgainstMediocrity.com/Resources
to download an editable PDF of the action items.

# CHAPTER 7

# YOU ARE A SALESPERSON

**Nothing happens in business until someone makes a sale.**

Merriam-Webster defines *sell* as "to persuade or influence to a course of action or the acceptance of something." Simply put, you are a salesperson. Everyone is in the sales profession.

Think back to when you were a child in the grocery store, when you wanted a piece of candy. Did you give up after the first "no?" As a child, the sales tactics you implemented were rudimentary, but you were, in fact, selling (persuading) your position to your mom for buying you candy. If you're married, you persuaded your spouse to marry you. If you're employed, you persuaded the owner to hire you. Whether you earn a commission or a salary, you are selling your services to your employer or customers. Have you ever eaten at an incredible restaurant or watched a spectacular movie, and you couldn't help but tell everyone about it? When you're discussing it, you persuade and influence everyone who listens to you to visit the restaurant or watch the movie. If you disagree with this chapter, you're probably thinking of reasons that will persuade me to believe you are not a salesperson, thus selling me on that point of view. *Selling* is a technical term for persuading, and we use it every day. Sales and selling often get a bad reputation because of pushy salespeople, but that is not selling. That is forcing.

## OWNERSHIP

Salespeople are told that they "eat what they kill," but for your ancestors, that phrase was literal. When cave people roamed the earth, survival was the only goal, and hunting was the only solution. Every day meant leaving the cave to find the next meal. In those days, the phrase "eat what you kill" meant life or death. They were wired to survive by any means necessary. No one would show up with a package of food to alleviate their hunger.

We all come pre-wired with our ancestors' survival instincts, which is why the unknown can be such a scary thing. It's scary to go "hunting" each morning and not know if you'll come home with anything for your family. What if you go too many days without bringing home food? You might have to move into the in-laws' cave! Sales and entrepreneurship can be unpredictable, and that increases your survival instincts: If you come home empty-handed, your days are numbered.

Fast-forward a few years to the 1800s, and the majority of people were still in the "eat what you kill" mentality. Everyone typically owned his or her own business and was required to sell or trade services with others to get wants and necessities. Common careers included farming, blacksmithing, butchering, bricklaying, carpentry, clock smithing, fishing, barbering, doctoring, teaching, publishing, and lawyering. Instead of getting a "job," most people became apprentices, assuming they'd eventually venture out on their own or assume the businesses of their teacher. That was the norm.

At some point along the line, entrepreneurs realized the power of a workforce and started hiring employees by the thousands. In exchange for labor, employees received commissions, a guaranteed amount every two weeks. Employment eliminated the fear of leaving the cave and coming home empty-handed. It provided the illusion of security in exchange for obeying orders. The fear of not surviving another day was gone in the eyes of the employee. Today's norm includes going to college and getting a good job, at a good company, with a good 401(k). Say goodbye to the "eat what you kill" mentality and replace it with "carnal security."

Employment to anyone but yourself breeds complacency. It's like an escalator that slowly takes you away from growth and progression. That's not to say you can't grow as an employee, but it involves an extreme intentional and proactive mindset. You have unlimited potential to do or become whatever you want, but if you settle for staying in the cave, you'll never know what you could have achieved.

Let me illustrate by telling a story. I'm the oldest of six siblings, and four of my siblings (including me) are married. Karlee, my sister, is thirteen months younger than me, and she was the first of my siblings to get married. My parents decided that, instead of paying for different aspects of the wedding, they would give Karlee a fixed dollar amount, and she and her future husband could decide what to do with it. Something amazing happened: Karlee decided on a very low-key wedding and kept nearly all the money. Since then, every married sibling has also received a fixed dollar amount and been given the choice of how to spend it. We've all followed in a similar fashion. If my parents had just paid for elements of the weddings, each of us would likely have made very different decisions. My dad has mentioned how differently my siblings and I spend, or don't spend, money when it's "our money." Ownership influences decision-making. When you "own it," you make different decisions than if someone else does.

The key is ownership. As a salesperson or entrepreneur, it's natural to take ownership because success is up to you. In what world does someone produce the same results every two weeks? It doesn't happen. Some weeks will be outstanding and others will be big, fat setbacks. If you get paid the same amount every two weeks, no matter your results, you're taught you don't need to take ownership. For me, it is demoralizing to be paid the same amount of money every two weeks when I know that some weeks I absolutely crushed it and earned well over a set salary, while other weeks I deserved nothing.

Even if you have a consistent paycheck right now, your employer could fire you tomorrow. The "safe" paycheck is your greatest weakness because it blinds you to potential downfalls. Look at yourself as a business: You, Inc. Work on and invest time into this business every day.

## SELL OR BE SOLD

Grant Cardone, in his book *Sell or Be Sold*, teaches that, at any moment, you are either selling or being sold, and everything in life is a commission. The definition of *commission*, according to Merriam-Webster, is a "fee paid to an agent or employee for transacting a piece of business or performing a service."

Let's say you set your alarm to wake up at 5:00 a.m. so you can get a head start on the day to change your life for the better. You decide to go to bed at 9:30 p.m. and are committed to waking up when the alarm goes off. Once the alarm sounds, you have two choices: stay in bed or get up and keep the commitment you made to yourself. The alarm starts screaming at 5:00 a.m. Let's imagine at that moment you have an angel version of yourself on one shoulder and a devil on the other. The angel tries to persuade you to wake up and accomplish your goals. On the other shoulder, the devil version tempts you to lay your head back down by whispering, "It's dark and cold outside. Stay in your bed where it is warm." Is this a familiar scenario? I know it has been for me. In this imaginary moment, you are being sold on whether to get out of bed or hit the snooze button. Your "commission" for getting out of bed will be improved health and confidence in yourself. Your commission for sleeping in will be frustration, delusion, and a loss of personal integrity.

Don't be sold on shortcuts and false narratives that limit your potential. Be sold on the fact that you can do anything. Be sold on your business, product, and dreams. Stop being sold on things that lead you toward mediocrity.

## FEAR AND REJECTION

One of the reasons most people avoid sales their entire lives is because it can be freaking scary. It is scary asking people for something, but that's the only way you'll ever get what you want in life! The truth is, the fear will never leave you. No matter your level of success, you will always encounter fear. The trick is not to "overcome" fear; "embrace" it!

The more frequently you embrace fear, the more accustomed you become to the emotions that accompany it. It is natural to be fearful, but it can cripple your growth if you don't quell it. It can prevent you from taking risks that could change your life. The following quote was mentioned earlier in the book, but Michael Jordan said it best: "Never say never, because limits, like fears, **are often just an illusion**." Fear is just an illusion. Think about it: How can one person be scared of spiders while another person will leap at the opportunity to have spiders crawl all over them. Fear is created in your mind. It isn't real.

The irony of fear is that it keeps you from starting. The hard and beautiful truth is that, when you start something new, you will suck at it. Guess what? That's okay! Don't let the fear of sucking keep you from starting! Everyone sucks when they start something new. Embrace the suck. Letting fear prevent you from starting will keep you from experiencing true joy. The pendulum of life swings in two directions: failure and success. You can only ever experience a monumental swing in success as high as your monumental swing in failure.

Rejection is often the stinging companion of sales. In the early days of civilization, rejection meant death. If you were rejected by and kicked out of the cave by your tribe, you were left alone to perish with the saber-tooth tigers. For this reason, we are each hard-wired with the innate fear of rejection. We want to be liked by those around us, which frequently leads to playing it safe.

I see too many people living below their potential simply because they are afraid of offending someone. The fear of rejection will never go away. You will always feel it. If you didn't feel fear, you would be a psychopath. You can, however, embrace rejection and learn to overcome it. The more you are rejected, the more you realize it won't kill you. In high school, I asked the same girl to three different dances, and she said no all three times! If I had given up on dating after those rejections, I would have never married my wife, Lauren. For that reason alone, I'm forever grateful I didn't give in to the fear of rejection. Just like in everyday life, experience in sales will help you become accustomed to fear and rejection. The best things in life are on the other side of fear.

## EMOTIONS ARE CONTAGIOUS

Have you ever walked into a room and immediately felt the heavy sensation of a recent argument? You can feel that, right? The same is true for an infectiously positive person: when you are around someone who exudes positivity, you feel happy. Why is that? It is because **emotions are contagious**.

Emotions spread faster than any virus, and only you can choose what emotions you will spread and tolerate in your life.

In a study done by researchers Nicholas Christakis and James Fowler, they found that "a person's happiness is related to the happiness of their friends, their friends' friends, and their friends' friends' friends—that is, to people well beyond their social horizon." When you tolerate negativity, it doesn't just affect you; It affects your friends, your friends' friends, and your friends' friends' friends. Talk about a pandemic of negativity, right?

Zig Ziglar says that sales is nothing more than the transfer of emotions. You'd be very surprised how much you can sell with no marketing material, a truckload of enthusiasm, and belief in your product. The opposite is true as well. If you are not 100% convinced that your product is the best thing for your customers, then your sales pitch has already failed. The emotions that come from a lack of confidence are transferred. So, sell something you believe in and then be unreasonably passionate about it. It must become your moral obligation to help people purchase your product because you believe it is the best thing for them. As long as you are continually adding value to others, there is no reason **not** to push for the sale persistently. If you can truly add value to someone's life, it is your obligation to do so.

## CREATE YOUR OWN ECONOMY

Sales ability allows you to no longer rely on market conditions. When you know how to sell, you can survive any economy. Let me repeat that: **when you know how to sell, you can survive any economy!** You control your future when you master the art of selling. The entire economy revolves around salespeople. Without them, inventors and business owners couldn't generate revenue from their products and services, accountants would have no money to count, manufacturers would have no orders, and there would be no need to store or ship products. Without salespeople, the economy would come to a grinding halt. Nothing happens in business or life until someone makes a sale. Even God and the devil need great salespeople.

Without the skill of sales, the winds of chance determine your course. You can't influence any outcomes in your life. As you choose to become a master of selling, you can gain unmatched wealth, freedom, influence, and success. There is no limit on your potential and the amount of good you can do for your family and community.

At some point, you will hear negative connotations about selling. We learned in Chapter 1 that what someone says reflects their beliefs. If someone speaks negatively about sales, they are reflecting their lack of knowledge and conviction around sales or negatives experiences they had in the past.

## BEST KNOWN, NOT BEST

In 2018, I started a new job selling homes, so Lauren and I moved back to the town we grew up in. A few friends from high school purchased homes from the company I worked for, but I wasn't the salesperson. I'm happy they purchased a home, but come on, I needed to be the one to help them. I also needed to provide for my family and hit my goals. Some people might have felt angry and placed blame, but I felt personally responsible for not getting the sales. I remembered learning from marketing experts that the best product doesn't win, the *best-known* product wins, like McDonald's. McDonald's is the largest burger chain in the world, but they do not make the best hamburger. They are, however, the best known: Everyone knows McDonald's.

From that point forward, I made a commitment to not just become the best, but the best known. To do this, I started posting on social media every day. At first it was very uncomfortable. I didn't like being vulnerable in front of people. Not only that, but I had gone about two years without using social media. At the time, it felt like a huge waste of time. Despite my trepidation, I continued to post. I posted about homes, success, The Fight Against Mediocrity, and lessons learned. Then, after about thirty days of posting every day, something amazing happened. Someone messaged me and thanked me for my posts. Then another, and another, and another. Not only were they thanking me, but they were supporting me and joining The Fight Against Mediocrity movement. While running errands, people I knew would walk up to me and say, "I didn't know you were so into self-development." Because I had never opened up and shared my message, no one knew. I started to experience the fruits of sharing my message and pushing to be the best known. Oh, and, yes, I started selling more homes as well.

## AGREE, AGREE, AGREE

The number one rule of sales is: "Always agree!" Why "always agree"? Because without agreement, there is no "agreement" or contract made. When I learned this principle, it completely changed my attitude and income. It makes complete sense: If I'm helping someone purchase a product or service and they tell me it's too expensive, why would I disagree with them? If I choose to say, "You're wrong, this is actually a great price," I just turned my customer into an enemy. I built a brick wall between myself and the customer. Humans are inherently very prideful, and we don't like to admit that we are wrong.

When you choose to "agree, agree, agree," you make friends and customers. Everyone wants to feel heard and understood. Until you let someone know you hear them, agree with them, and see their point of view, they'll never turn into a paying customer. It sounds bizarre. For example, if someone tells me that my price is too high, I respond confidently, "You're totally right, it is a high price, I agree with you." Guess what happens after that? THEY BUY MY PRODUCT OR SERVICE! Try this in all aspects of your life: with your kids, your wife, your friends, your family, and community members. Choose to "always agree." You want those around you to think, "Wow, they get me."

Grant Cardone has a challenge called The Agreement Challenge. Try agreeing with everything and everyone around you for twenty-four hours. If you mess up, start over. It's much harder than you think.

## LINDA, LISTEN!

Most people listen to respond, not to understand. Let me explain. During a discussion, instead of listening to the other person, you are thinking about what you will say next. But wait. How can you know what to say without listening and understanding the other person? Now you see the problem. As the late Stephen Covey said, "Seek to understand, then to be understood." Without truly understanding those with whom you are speaking, you are unable to help them. We innately understand this. For example, a doctor must ask questions and understand the needs of the patient to give the correct diagnosis. Despite its simplicity, it is extremely difficult to master.

To make matters even more difficult, the words someone speaks are only 7% of what they are truly saying. A study conducted by Dr. Albert Mehrabian at UCLA discovered the 7/38/55 rule. The rule suggests that 7% of communication is in the words we speak, 38% is our tone of voice, and 55% is in our bodies and posture. I know you've experienced a situation when someone says one thing, but their body language and tone of voice are saying the complete opposite. If you can't see the other person, it is absolutely critical to listen at full capacity. In fact, in his book *Never Split the Difference*, Chris Voss explains that, in FBI hostage situations, they have up to five people listening to a kidnapper, ten ears all focused on picking up any clue that could give them an advantage. You only have two ears, and it's not cost-effective to hire five people to listen in on all your conversations. This means you must dial in and focused whenever you are in a conversation. Otherwise, you will miss out on what the other person is truly saying.

Too often, salespeople feel like they need to "throw up" all the features of the product on the customer. A paradox of life is that the more you listen to the customer, the more likely they are sold on the product or service. Let's go back to the example of the doctor. If you walk into a doctor's office and he or she immediately prescribes you medicine without asking a single question and proceeds to tell you why it's the best medicine on the market, "with cutting-edge features and benefits," are you going to use the medicine? I highly doubt it. The doctor doesn't even know why you are in the office in the first place. They didn't ask! You will feel pressured, uncomfortable, and unsure of the doctor's abilities. The same is true in sales. Being pushy without first listening to the customer will only cause issues in the sales process, no matter how good your product or service is. Seek to understand then to be understood.

Great listeners also ask great questions. The fundamental issues you need to uncover in a sales conversation are **why do they want the product or service, why today, and what do they currently have to solve the problem, or do they have anything at all?** You'll get all the information you need and more from just those three questions.

Here are a few tips to make sure you are listening to your customers. Your customers might be your spouse, children, parents, coworkers, boss, etc.:

- Never interrupt. Always pause before responding to make sure they are finished speaking.
- Always, always, always, agree.
- Ask meaningful questions that cause your customer to think. (Avoid yes or no questions.)
- Understand your customer's true motivation.

- Don't think about your response until your customer is done speaking.
- Say, "Tell me more," to make sure they've said everything they want to.
- Don't be afraid of silence. Embrace it.
- Ask one question and then be silent; don't ramble.
- Focus not just on the words they speak but the tone of voice and body language.

At the end of the day, your conversation partner knows whether or not you are truly listening to them. I know because, even when I'm on the phone with my wife, Lauren, she will call me out. She knows if I'm engaged or not, even if she can't see my body language. Do yourself a favor and learn to be a great active listener.

## ALWAYS ASK FOR THE SALE

Most people lose the sale before they even start selling. How? They never ask for the sale. This typically stems from fear of rejection, but let's be real: the worst thing that can happen is they say no. That is literally the worst thing that can happen. I've never read a headline that says someone was tortured to death with *no*s. A *no* won't kill you. In fact, everything you want in life is on the other side of no.

One of the biggest mistake's parents are making across the globe is teaching their kids to avoid strangers. Why? Strangers have everything they want/need in life. Your customers are strangers before you get to know them. In fact, when you were born, everyone was a stranger, even your parents and the nurse that pulled you into this world. If you avoided strangers, you wouldn't be here, and you wouldn't have a family. Of course, you shouldn't walk up to a man in a dark alley, but "strangers" have everything you want in life. To start a business, meet and convince strangers to buy from you.

When I was in my early teens, my parents took me to a financial class at a local theater in our area. I only remember one lesson from that event, but it made me $10,000 later down the road. They taught us that, whenever you are purchasing something, to ask the question, "Is that the best you can do?" referring to the price. It was a magical question that brought discounts galore. I started using it from that point forward and frequently got a better deal just by using those seven words. When negotiating my first salary position upon graduating college, I remember I was driving down I-15 near Provo, Utah, and my soon-to-be boss told me the salary they were offering me. I calmly asked, "Is that the best you can do?" She immediately said they could raise it by $10,000, but that was the highest they could do. Boom, $10,000 raise! If I had never asked, I would have never received the increased offer. Ask, ask, ask! The worst they can say is no. Everything in life is negotiable, and strangers have everything you want. A customer should never leave without your asking for the sale.

Asking helps you in everything in your life. Just recently, my wife and I were at a party. They didn't have the food we wanted, so we walked to a nearby restaurant. It was a Friday night, and the wait was over two hours! I asked if we could order something to-go, and the waitress said we could go downstairs and order something. After our food arrived, I asked if we could sit outside and eat, and the waitress said yes. So, we ended up eating at the restaurant, outside under the stars, in just twenty minutes. Don't settle for the first no. Keep asking for the sale. **Never lose a sale because you didn't ask.**

## FOLLOW-UP AND PERSISTENCE

Once you've asked for the sale, you will realize that you hear a lot of nos. Welcome to sales. My friend Jeb Blount says that, if sales were easy, everyone would be doing it and be getting paid minimum wage. The great news is that the numbers reveal 50% of sales are made after the fifth contact, and 92% of salespeople give up after no sales on the fourth call. This gives you an immediate unfair advantage over other salespeople. Don't give up. Follow up when others won't. The average sales rep makes only two attempts to reconnect with a prospect. This is one of the reasons why there is often a very high turnover rate in sales. They fail to follow-up and give up too quickly. Here are the stats according to Zoom Info:

- 50% of sales happen after the 5th contact.
- The average sales rep only makes 2 attempts to reach a prospect.
- 44% of salespeople give up after one follow-up.
- 92% of salespeople give up after no sales on the 4th call, while 60% of customers say no four times before saying yes.
- 75% of online buyers want to receive between 2-4 phone calls before a company gives up; 12% would like a company to try as many times as it takes to get a hold of them.

I consider follow-up to be the closest thing to "sales magic" that there is. While selling SAAS (software as a service) products, I experienced this phenomenon every week because I was relentless in my follow-up. Someone was always unavailable, so I'd call them every single day for a few weeks. I remember one person who had been especially difficult to contact. I'd called him close to fifteen times at this point with only one response. Finally, he answered, and within thirty minutes, he'd signed up for the service like it was nothing. It was "sales magic!" This happens all the time! It is crazy how simple it is. I like to say that the most persistent bird gets the worm every time.

This applies to every aspect of life, not just sales. If you truly want something in life, it will rarely come on the first, second, or even third try. It will usually happen after a dozen or maybe even hundreds of attempts. The Stonecutters Credo displays a perfect example of the power of persistence: Jacob Riis said, "When nothing seems to help, I go and look at a stonecutter hammering away at his rock perhaps a hundred times without as much as a crack showing in it. Yet at the hundred and first blow it will split in two, and I know it was not that blow that did it, but all that had gone before."

## SELLING IS SERVING

*Service* as defined by Merriam-Webster is, "contribution to the welfare of others." If you provide a quality product or service that adds value to people's lives and you believe in it, it is your responsibility and moral obligation to sell, expand, and grow. Your product or service does no good in your mind or in your warehouse; it must be in the hands of your customer. The only people who won't take their business from $100,000 to $10,000,000 or even $1,000,000,000 are selfish. Unselfish people grow their businesses, influences, and sales. Selfish people only produce what they need. Why do unselfish people grow more and more? They do it so they can take care of their family, friends, and community during any economy. They expand to leave a legacy and change the world!

You serve a customer when you exchange your product or service for money. The exchange of money is necessary. Nothing worth having in life is free. You value things differently when you make a purchase rather than receiving it. You value what you pay for. Otherwise, why would you buy it? I learned this from my good friend Roger Comstock. Your customers will value what you sell more when they pay the full price. Do not give discounts on your products or services. Customers often have a difficult time gauging the value of what you are selling, so they use the price to determine value. If you sell a product for $1,000 and then discount $500 from the price because you think it will get your potential customer off the fence, you are dead wrong! For most customers it will raise suspicion of what you are selling. Customers will ask themselves, "What's wrong with it? Why are they giving me a discount?" Those that buy because of a discount will require significant maintenance and never see the value in what you are providing. In all my experience, I have found that the best customers pay full price.

When you give discounts during the sales process, you are doing you, your company, and your customer a disservice. **Nothing in life worth having is free.** Everything worth having has a price. Your health has a price; it's called healthy food and exercise. Your relationships have a price: time and love. Your emotional and mental health have a price. Success has a price. Freedom has a price.

In case you think I'm blowing smoke, I'll share two stories about the importance of never giving discounts. I began selling a home to a middle-aged couple, but they couldn't decide which lot they wanted. One of their preferred properties had a $7,000 discount. To give some context, every lot in each community has a premium or a discount depending on size, direction the house will face, slope, etc. This specific lot was smaller than the other lots in the community. The soil and all other aspects of the lot were in excellent condition, but because of the discount, the buyer leaned forward and with great concern in her voice and asked, "What is wrong with the lot? I don't want to buy a lot that has something wrong with it." She raised this concern based solely on the price. Price was directly related to the value of the property. The best thing we could have done was remove the discount from the lot.

She's not alone. Your customers will value your product to the extent of your price. Customers don't buy based on what the price is (have you ever said something cost too much money but then purchased it anyway?); they buy with their emotions and then justify it with logic.

My second experience happened while selling software products. I had followed up several times with a business in

Wyoming and was finally able to reach the owner. He really wanted to purchase the product but said the price was too high, and I made the mistake of starting down the road of giving a discount. (Price was not the issue; seeing enough value in the product was his issue.) A few discounts later, he eventually purchased the platform for two of his business locations. He became one of the worst customers we had. It wasn't necessarily because he was a mean person but because he never used the platform! Our customer success team called him consistently, but he never took the time to set up the platform. He didn't pay the full price and, for that reason, didn't see the value in spending time using it.

If you believe in what you do and believe you are the best at what you do, you now have a duty, a responsibility to yourself and your customer, to ensure they have access to your product or service. It is a disservice for them to walk away without your product or service. If you never come to an agreement with a customer, you lose, and they lose.

**CONCLUSION**

During this chapter, you may have felt this applied immediately to your situation or that I was way off base. If you didn't feel like it applied, I invite you to reread it. Everyone is a salesperson. The principles in this chapter translate into everything you do. Even if you are currently in a position where you never speak to a customer, you are still selling your services to a business. If you are a spouse or parent, you are constantly persuading your wife and children to do or not to do something. The first step is realizing you are a salesperson. The next step is committing to becoming great at sales.

Need motivation and more help? Scan the QR code to access free resources including my favorite motivational videos.

**CHAPTER SEVEN - YOU ARE A SALESPERSON**

# TAKE ACTION
## NOTHING CHANGES UNLESS SOMETHING CHANGES

- **Emotions are contagious.** Write down what emotions you want to transfer to others.
- Always follow up at least **twelve times**.
- **Always ask for the sale** (ask for what you want).
- Make a commitment to become great at sales.
- **Post daily on social media** and become known in your industry as an expert.
- If you'd like to learn about how to make six figures in sales visit www.TheFightAgainstMediocrity.com.

# FREE
# ADDITIONAL
# RESOURCES

or visit TheFightAgainstMediocrity.com/Resources to download an editable PDF of the action items.

# CHAPTER 8

---

## PRICELESS

**"I've learned that people will forget what you said, people will forget what you did, but people will never forget how you made them feel." —Maya Angelou**

From a young age, most of what you learned was developed through mimicking the people around you. Humans mimic. If you've ever said a four-letter word around a child, you know exactly what I mean. You, me, and everyone absorbs information around us and models it in our own lives, consciously or subconsciously. If you hang out with people who like to party, you will party. If you hang out with people who like to skateboard, you will learn to skateboard. If you hang out with people who like to . . . well, I think you get the point. Even the latest fashion styles come from mimicking trendsetters. One of my best friends wore a shoelace as a belt in high school, so what did my other friends and I end up doing? Yep, you guessed it. We wore shoelaces as belts. My wife still teases me about it to this day. Humans desire acceptance and inclusion in a community. Humans not only thrive on community and connection. It is a necessity. You are a product of the people surrounding you. That's not my opinion; it's a fact.

## SHOW ME YOUR FRIENDS, I'LL SHOW YOU YOUR FUTURE

You may have heard that you are the product of the five people with whom you spend the most time. Well, it's true. This is great news, but also terrifying news. One of the quickest ways to radically transform your life is to get around the right people or remove the wrong people. Let me share an example in my life.

I competed as a professional unicyclist from ages sixteen to nineteen. Super random, I know. At the time I stopped unicycling (because my ankles always took beatings and I wanted to be able to walk with my grandkids), I was ranked 2nd in North America and 4th in the world, but it didn't start like that. One thing changed everything for me and took me from mediocre to the top 1% of unicyclists in the world!

I started unicycling when I was eleven years old. From the ages of twelve to fifteen, I could only land two tricks and had never competed in a unicycle event. I dreamed of landing the tricks I saw my favorite riders land on YouTube, but I just couldn't seem to figure them out. It definitely wasn't due to a lack of practice, because I unicycled two to four hours every day. I should have felt good about myself because, out of the thirty unicyclists in my high school club (yeah, we had a unicycle club), I was the best. That's the thing, though: I didn't just want to be the best in my community. I wanted to be the best in the world.

At age fifteen, I decided to go to NAUCC (North America Unicycle Competition and Convention) in South Dakota. What I didn't realize was that the next week in South Dakota would change my unicycle career. I learned from the top unicyclists in the world. I pestered them with questions and asked them to critique my techniques. I surrounded myself with the best unicyclists in the world. For one week, they were the five people I spent the most time with.

Fast-forward two years from that competition in South Dakota, and I placed 5th place in the Street Competition in Madison, Wisconsin, at NAUCC. I went from just two tricks to over one hundred. I went from no competitions to 5th place in North America just two years later! Shortly after that, I was sponsored by the best unicycle maker in the world, Kris Holm Unicycles, and FiveTen shoe company. In 2014, I was featured in a DevinSuperTramp YouTube video with over two million views. So, what made the difference?

My proximity to the best unicyclists in the world in South Dakota and in the years that followed made all the difference. It was the game changer that took me from mediocre to the top 1% in the world. Proximity is the primary thing that will take you from where you are now to where you want to go in your self-development and future. Reading books and watching videos will only take you so far. You can't put a price tag on getting around the right people and the right information! Who do you need to get around to change your situation? What will it cost to get around them? Do you need to get a new job? Move to a new city? Pay to attend a mastermind? Whatever you need to do, *do it*! Sometimes you need to pay to play. Fortunately for me, my parents were kind enough to help me attend NAUCC, but since then, I've paid tens of thousands of dollars to get around the right people to take me to the next level in my career and personal development. The biggest mistake I've made was thinking that I was paying for information when I attended a conference, mastermind, workshop, or training. You're paying for the connections and the network. Like they say, your "network equals your net worth," and not just your monetary worth. This includes your health and wellness.

As you analyze the goals, you're setting for yourself, include your associations to achieve them. With technology, there is no excuse for not getting around the people, either digitally or in person, who will take you to the next level.

Pay close attention to whom you follow on social media. It might seem harsh, but if you are following someone and what they post isn't helping you reach your potential, unfollow them. It might be your friends from high school or even your siblings, but I promise it will be a breath of fresh air to get rid of the negativity.

## WHERE TO FIND HAPPINESS

The reasons for health and happiness are often long and drawn-out conversations. Despite the depth of the topic, we can learn a good amount from Bugs Bunny. Well, maybe not Bugs Bunny himself, but some of his relatives. In a discourse given by Gary E. Stevenson, he shares a story about a study done on rabbits that teaches us one way to achieve more happiness in our lives:

> "In the 1970s, researchers set up an experiment to examine the effects of diet on heart health. Over several months, they fed a control group of rabbits a high-fat diet and monitored their blood pressure, heart rate, and cholesterol.

As expected, many of the rabbits showed a buildup of fatty deposits on the inside of their arteries. Yet this was not all! Researchers had discovered something that made little sense. Although all of the rabbits had a buildup, one group surprisingly had as much as 60 percent less than the others. It appeared as though they were looking at two different groups of rabbits.

To scientists, results like this can cause lost sleep. How could this be? The rabbits were all the same breed from New Zealand, from a virtually identical gene pool. They each received equal amounts of the same food.

What could this mean?

Did the results invalidate the study? Were there flaws in the experiment design?

The scientists struggled to understand this unexpected outcome!

Eventually, they turned their attention to the research staff. Was it possible that researchers had done something to influence the results? As they pursued this, they discovered that every rabbit with fewer fatty deposits had been under the care of one researcher. She fed the rabbits the same food as everyone else. But, as one scientist reported, "she was an unusually kind and caring individual." When she fed the rabbits, "she talked to them, cuddled and petted them. . . . "She couldn't help it. It's just how she was."

She did more than simply give the rabbits food. She gave them love!

At first glance, it seemed unlikely that this could be the reason for the dramatic difference, but the research team could see no other possibility.

So they repeated the experiment—this time tightly controlling for every other variable. When they analyzed the results, the same thing happened! **The rabbits under the care of the loving researcher had significantly higher health outcomes.**

The scientists published the results of this study in the prestigious journal *Science*."

Everyone needs love, community, friendship, and kindness. No matter the race, nationality, religious background, EVERYONE NEEDS LOVE. For whatever reason, some people hold back praise, love, and admiration for others. Spread love like it's a hot potato directly out of the oven. The irony is that the people who say they don't want love are the ones that need it the most. We are all dealing with crap, and we've all got weaknesses. Jesus Christ said it plain and simple when he boldly declared: **"Thou shalt love thy neighbour as thyself."**

In my final class of the Masters of Real Estate Development program at The University of Utah, my professor, Flyn had just undergone chemotherapy for cancer and looked very fragile and worn from the treatments. Despite all of this, he taught via video conference, and you could tell he loved it. One day, during class, he stopped mid-sentence and asked one of my classmates to show the class more of her newborn daughter who she was holding. He said, "It will help us remember what is most important and what is trivial." That hit me hard. Flyn was going through a battle with cancer, and he taught me and my five classmates the most important lesson we'd learned in the entire graduate program. He had been through hell, and it was very obvious that he had become infinitely aware of what was most important in life. People are the most important. Relationships will always trump anything else. Flyn passed away just a few weeks after he made that statement. I learned two incredible lessons from Flyn: The first is the importance of relationships and people. Never let work, school, or life get in the way of strengthening and cultivating love in your relationships. The second is the importance of giving back and leaving a legacy. During Flyn's class, it was very apparent that he was taking medication and struggling through the pain. Despite the pain and the difficulties he was experiencing, it was obvious he loved what he was doing. He loved teaching and giving back. Teaching wasn't his profession—he was a VP at a large bank—but teaching was his way of helping those around him become better. None of us know how much longer we will be on Earth, but we all know that, at some point, it will come to an end. Make every day count by investing in your relationships and giving back to your friends, family, community, and church.

Let's say you were the most famous person in the world, had all the money in the world, and had every worldly possession you've dreamed of. Heck, let's even throw in that you have the perfect physique as well. You now have everything that most people spend all their time dreaming about. Here is the catch: you are the only person on planet Earth. You have the mansion, Lamborghini, and jet, but no one to share it with. I bet that, within a very short period of time, you'd give it all up if you could have just one friend to cherish and love. Don't get me wrong, I love the pursuit of goals, ambitions, and dreams more than anyone else. That's a large portion of what I've talked about in this book. We need money to live, so to denounce it would be foolish, but that's not the point. The point is relationships, love, and leaving a legacy for future generations.

Harvard conducted a study with 268 sophomores and followed them over the span of 80 years. The intent of the study was to determine causes for health and happiness. The outcomes of the study are summed up in the following quotes by those involved:

> "When we gathered together everything we knew about them at age fifty, it wasn't their middle-age cholesterol levels that predicted how they were going to grow old. It was how satisfied they were in their relationships. The people who were the most satisfied in their relationships at age fifty were the healthiest at age eighty." —Robert Waldinger

> "When the study began, nobody cared about empathy . . . But the key to healthy aging is relationships, relationships, relationships." — George Vaillant

Relationships fall into the category of Important but Not Urgent. If you choose to skip date night with your loved one for just one week, it's not going to end in divorce. If you choose not to play with your children for a few days, no big deal; they'll forgive you. The real kicker comes over time when relationships are neglected and priorities are skewed. Years of neglect are difficult and nearly impossible to repair. You need to make a daily and weekly commitment to improve your relationships because they can't be last-minute thoughts, and they definitely can't be fixed with a Band-Aid-type solution.

## PRICELESS MARRIAGE

At the time I'm writing this book, seven of the ten wealthiest people in the world are divorced. Bill and Melinda Gates just announced their divorce, which made them the seventh. If you count Warren Buffet and his wife's short-lived separation, then it jumps to eight out of ten. If eight out of ten of the wealthiest people in the world have broken marriages, it begs the question, what went wrong? Should you rush to the bank and give all your money to charity for the fear of divorce? Hold your horses; let's dive into this. I've never met any of these people, so for me to say why their marriages ended in divorce is speculation. So that's exactly what I'm going to do: speculate. I believe that people don't fall in and out of love. Love is a verb, and verbs require action. So, if you want your marriage brimming with love, it needs to include a lot of action. Make time to create memories every week. Don't take the little things for granted. Show love for one another. Agree on times and locations in your home where work and technology are not allowed. It takes discipline and effort to create anything great, and that includes a great marriage.

**"No other success can compensate for failure in the home."**
**—David O. McKay**

I've learned two great lessons about marriage from success expert Darren Hardy: According to Hardy, a marriage isn't a 50/50 effort. It is a 0/100 effort. You are responsible for giving 100% to the marriage, no matter what. We've already gone over this in Chapter 1: You can't control your significant other. You can only control you! Hardy also shared the story that he wrote down one thing he was grateful for about his wife every day for a year. He said it is now her most cherished gift, and to his surprise, his love grew each day as he noticed the little things she did.

One day I came home excited to share a new goal I had made with Lauren. I sat her down and exclaimed, "I want to have a billion-dollar marriage."

"What does that mean?" she responded, very confused.

"Well, to be a billionaire is to win at the game of money, and I want to win in our marriage, so it made sense in my head that we should aim for a billion-dollar marriage."

I'll never forget what Lauren said after that. With a calm voice she taught me, "We don't want a billion-dollar marriage. We want a priceless marriage."

Lauren proceeded to tell me how she learned her definition of the word *priceless*. When she was in elementary school, a boy teased her, calling her "priceless." She assumed it meant something mean and was devastated. The teacher then explained to her that it was a good thing, and it meant that something was so valuable it couldn't be purchased with money. That's exactly how a marriage should be. Something that is valuable requires constant work, love, and support.

If you don't have a spouse, here's one piece of advice: You don't find a great spouse; you attract a great spouse by the person you are. If you find the "perfect" spouse, what makes you think they'd want to marry you? When I was twenty-three years old, I wrote down a one-page list of attributes I would strive to become, and I read it every morning for two years. Each day I would adjust my attitudes and behaviors to become the person I had written down on the paper. Two years later, Lauren and I started dating, and she is everything on the list. Intentionality is the key.

## BE A BUILDER

When I graduated college, I moved to Salt Lake City, Utah. I didn't have any friends in the area. So, what did I do? I started introducing myself to people at the gym. One morning, I ran into an acquaintance I'd met while I was a freshman in college, Jer (Jeremy). As is typical with gym bros, we worked out together every morning with his buddy J (Jason). Jer, J, and I became extremely good friends. One morning, I came into the gym a little hotheaded and said something sarcastic to J. Jer stopped abruptly and said, "Kevin, we are builders. We build people up." It was his constant reminder. "We are builders. We build people up." Ever since then, it's stuck with me, and I love the emotion it carries. Building people up makes you feel good, and it's a worthy cause. It's something worth fighting for. I know for me, I'd rather spend time with people who build me up with what they say and do.

## THE THREE-MINUTE RULE

Lauren and I attended a conference with speaker Jesse Itzler. I'd heard of Jesse but never really listened to any of his content. It was inspiring to say the least. We ended up running into him after the conference, and despite a near car accident, we snagged this picture with him.

He mentioned "The Three-Minute Rule" during the conference, and it bears repeating. Essentially, take just three minutes each day and send a few messages thanking people. Yeah, it's that simple. Despite its incredible simplicity and happy returns, it also makes the recipients feel great. I took the challenge and started taking three minutes every day to thank people. It's fun to say thank you and see how big an impact such a small habit can make.

Give it a try. It only takes three minutes.

## PAY TO PLAY

Speaking of conferences, even after the experience I had during my first unicycle competition in South Dakota, I was reluctant to spend my own money on conferences and events. It was easy to go to South Dakota when my dad was paying, but I struggled to fork over the money. There were several business conferences I really wanted to attend, but if it wasn't an incredibly good deal, I'd talk myself out of it or just wait to buy the recording. I believed the recording would be just as beneficial, and that way I didn't have to spend money on travel. I figured I could watch it at my own leisure, and I could replay it multiple times. Even though it makes sense logically, I was sorely mistaken! I had forgotten that the greatest benefit of attending conferences, workshops, boot camps, and trainings isn't for the material, it's for the *people*! This entire chapter is about relationships, but more importantly, it's about the *right* relationships. It took me longer than it should have, but I finally realized that, by attending a conference, I'm making a commitment backed by time, money, and energy. Everyone else in attendance is doing the same thing. It's the unspoken commitment that each person shows when attending that make the connections so powerful. Pay whatever it takes to get around the right people who are equipped to take you to your desired destination. This is one of the paradoxes of life: to make more money, you must spend money to get around the right people. No event will ever charge too much as long as you take advantage and grow your network. You can probably find ways to get into rooms without paying. You could be the server at the table or an employee for the venue. Either way, get around the right people.

In Napoleon Hill's best-selling book *Think and Grow Rich*, he calls the connection with the right people a "Mastermind." In his words, the reason "great power can be accumulated through no other principle" other than a Mastermind is: "people take on the nature and the habits and the power of thought of those with whom they associate in a spirit of sympathy and harmony." In layman's terms, "You become like the people you spend time with."

The mastermind principle is fascinating because one plus one doesn't equal two. The combined effort, knowledge, and energy of two people is greater than the sum. This phenomenon is illustrated perfectly by Belgian draft horses. A single horse can pull a weight of approximately eight thousand pounds, but two horses don't pull sixteen thousand pounds — they pull twenty-two thousand. Not only that, but if two horses train together frequently, they can pull up to thirty-two thousand pounds. If you get around the right people, your individual knowledge is multiplied. The opposite is true as well. Spend too much time with the wrong people, and your previous efforts will fade and eventually disappear.

**THERE IS NO SUCH THING AS A SELF-MADE MAN OR WOMAN**

The lie that some people are self-made is making the rounds. There is actually no such thing as a self-made man. Everyone receives help along the way. I learned this lesson from Arnold Schwarzenegger. If you know Arnold's story, you might think that he is the exact definition of a self-made person! He came from Austria to California all alone where he went on to not only become the youngest person to win Mr. Olympia, but to win it seven times. After that, he became the highest-paid actor in Hollywood! Then he put the cherry on top by becoming the governor of California!

Why did Arnold say, despite all of his accomplishments and hard work, that there is no such thing as a self-made man? First of all, he was inspired to come to America to become a bodybuilder and actor by Roy "Reg" Park. Arnold didn't come up with that vision by himself: he was inspired by Reg. When arriving in California, he was warmly welcomed and met people who helped him progress in a new country. His in-laws were members of the Kennedy family and inspired him to get into politics. Everything he did and accomplished was inspired by others, and he had so many people who supported him along the way.

A side note on Arnold: he wasn't sure what he wanted to do until he saw a magazine with Roy "Reg" Park. At that point, everything became possible. Reg became a part of his circle, just by reading about him. We can also add people to our circles by reading, listening to, and watching others' content. If you can't spend time with and learn from someone personally, dive into their content, and you'll start to think and act like them.

If Arnold needed help along the way, then I guarantee that you'll need some help along the way as well. Ask for help, but more importantly, accept the help you're offered. After that, give back and pass it forward.

Another paradox of life is that you receive more by giving than you do by receiving. In Jon Huntsman Sr.'s book *Barefoot to Billionaire*, he describes a time when he had nothing. As a newly married couple, Jon and his wife barely earned enough money to cover household expenses. Despite following their budget, they were consistently short $100 every month. Jon had been giving $100 to a widow in their neighborhood every month, even though he knew it would leave his family's budget short $100. If you aren't familiar with Jon Huntsman, he is one of the most generous individuals in Utah and the world. He has given away amounts totaling well over a billion dollars, and his foundation continues to provide support around the world, even after his passing. His goal was to eradicate cancer, and he is well known for funding the Huntsman Cancer Institute in Salt Lake City, Utah. Here is the underlying lesson: If you aren't willing to give when you have nothing, you will not give when you have everything. **Money doesn't change you. It only amplifies who you already are**. Read that again.

## LEAVING A LEGACY

Everyone wants to be remembered. I'm sure the idea of leaving a legacy, something bigger than yourself, has crossed your mind. Leaving a legacy is the reason for big hospitals with patrons' names on them. It's why a university can ask for large sums of money to build a new facility with only the exchange of a name on a building or room. Part of this motivation comes from status, ego, and pride. Another part comes from giving back because of your gifts. This motivation is in your DNA. The mammalian limbic system releases chemicals that make you happy when you do things that promote reproductive success, like having children, putting your name on a building, leaving a foundation of money, etc.

What legacy do you want to leave for your family, friends, neighbors, and the world? How do you want to be remembered? You are going to leave a legacy; it is inevitable and unavoidable. The question is, what will it be? Who will it impact and how? Why is it important to you? Ask yourself the question, what do you want said about you at your funeral? Once you've answered these questions, all that's left is to live each day until it becomes a reality.

> "If you live each day as if it were your last, someday you'll be right. Every morning I looked in the mirror and asked myself: 'If today were the last day of my life, would I want to do what I am about to do today?'" —Steve Jobs

Need motivation and more help? Scan the QR code to access free resources including my favorite motivational videos.

CHAPTER EIGHT - PRICELESS

# TAKE ACTION
**NOTHING CHANGES UNLESS SOMETHING CHANGES**

- Sign up for a conference or mastermind.
- Answer these questions about leaving a legacy:
  - What legacy will you leave for your family, friends, and the world?
  - What do you want to be said about you at your funeral?
- **Make it a priority to spend quality time with your family.**
- Make a list of attributes you desire your future spouse to have and work every day to cultivate them in yourself.
- Serve a friend or neighbor.
- Scan the QR code to take the "influence test."

# FREE ADDITIONAL RESOURCES

or visit TheFightAgainstMediocrity.com/Resources
to download an editable PDF of the action items.

# CHAPTER 9

---

# NEVER GIVE UP

**"Real courage is holding on to a still voice in your head that says, "I must keep going." It's that voice that says nothing is a failure if it is not final—that voice that says to you, "Get out of bed. Keep going. I will not quit." —Cory Booker**

You fail if you never start. Once you've started, you only fail if you quit. Merriam-Webster defines *fail* as: "to lose strength, to fade or die away, or to fall short." This definition feels like it casts a negative light on failure, but it's actually the opposite. Growth and strength come after and during failure, not before. Failing and "losing strength" is common when you're at the gym and you push as hard as you can until the very last rep. You pushed yourself to "failure." After failure is where the magic starts to happen. The process is called *muscle hypertrophy*, when the fibers of the muscles are damaged. The body starts to repair the torn fibers by fusing them, which increases the mass and size of the muscles. The initial tearing sustained by pushing the muscle to failure was the catalyst for eventually increasing its strength and size. Failure has become taboo, but it is actually essential to helping you grow and become better.

It might sound weird for me to say, but you must first be mediocre before eventually becoming excellent. Your goal is to fight mediocrity, but that doesn't mean you're not mediocre when you're first starting out.

We are all conditioned from our first days in school to think that failure is a bad thing and should be avoided at all costs. Students who fail are labeled as slow or unintelligent. Fast-forward twenty years from first grade, and this mindset has stuck with you; it's difficult to shake. The irony is that, to succeed, you must go through failure, not around or over it. For this reason, it is absolutely necessary to embrace failure! Albert Einstein said, "Anyone who has never made a mistake has never tried anything new."

Persisting, despite making mistakes, is an inherent trait. When you learned to walk, it only came after hundreds, maybe thousands, of failed attempts. After each attempt, you would make tiny adjustments and become stronger until one day you were able to walk, then eventually run. Pluck the idea of avoiding failure from your brain and replace it with cherishing setbacks and failures. If failing is "to fade or die away," then the only way you will fail is if you stop trying.

If you stay in the game every day, you will never fail permanently. The key is to embrace temporary failures, adjust, learn from what did or didn't work, and then try again. Tennis player Billie Jean King said, "Champions keep playing until they get it right."

Go for failure in everything you do, then keep trying until you get it right! Growth can only occur after failure. Let's take weightlifting for example again: Your goal is to take the muscles to failure and then keep pushing. It's only after failure that the muscle fibers break and grow stronger. Too many people are easily lifting metaphorical five-pound weights instead of pushing themselves to failure. Embrace the big red F that teachers taught you to abhor. Michael Jordan once said, "I've missed more than nine thousand shots in my career. I've lost almost three hundred games. Twenty-six times I've been trusted to take the game-winning shot and missed. I've failed over and over and over again in my life. THAT IS WHY I SUCCEED."

Do you get it? Do you realize how messed up your view of failure has been from a young age? Is your paradigm starting to shift? It will take weeks, months, and maybe even years to rewire your brain to **love failing**. Every "failure" is a step toward success.

"I had a mother who taught me there is no such thing as failure. It is just a temporary postponement of success." —Buddy Ebsen

Most people fear failure. Unfortunately, avoiding failure leads to failure. Jim Carrey shared a story about his father in the quote below:

"Many of us choose our path out of fear disguised as practicality. What we really want seems impossibly out of reach and ridiculous to expect, so we never dare to ask the universe for it. My father could've been a great comedian, but he didn't believe that that was possible for him, and so he made a conservative choice . . . he got a safe job as an accountant, and when I was twelve years old, he was let go from that safe job, and our family had to do whatever we could to survive. I learned many great lessons from my father, not the least of which was that you can fail at what you don't want, so you might as well take a chance on doing what you love."

That's why I am writing this book. Since I can remember, I wanted to be a motivator, a leader, a speaker, and a source of inspiration and good for others. I've always felt the deep desire to Fight Mediocrity and help others do the same. If this book flops, I will try again and again until I succeed. I know that I will never fail as long as I don't quit.

## MORE VALUABLE THAN GOLD

In the moment, failure seems like our own personal Mount Everest that is looming over us and mocking our abilities. It feels insurmountable and impossible. The time frame of failure can seem never-ending. Despite this, remember that every time your life rollercoaster goes down, it will go back up again. Failure breeds success, and it is in the hardest moments that you learn the most. It is in your moments of weakness that you are humble enough to try something new and make dramatic changes in your life. I've come to learn that to be at rock bottom and to have your back against a wall is actually a blessing. It's impossible to replicate that feeling, and when you are in that moment, you will have some of your greatest sparks of inspiration and creativity.

In Peter 1:7 (KJV), it says, "That the trial of your faith, being much **more precious than of gold that perisheth**, though it be tried with fire, might be found unto **praise and honour and glory** at the appearing of Jesus Christ." I love this scripture, and no matter what religion you do or don't subscribe to, there are some gold nuggets in these words.

**First, trials are more valuable than gold!** At the time, gold had the highest value of any currency. The scripture signified to the reader that, instead of seeking after gold, they should seek opportunities for growth. Trials and challenges are typically imposed by forces outside our control, but the most successful people in the world create *self-imposed challenges*. Self-imposed challenges are hiring a personal trainer to push you further than you previously thought possible, going to an event that is more money than you have in your bank account, setting Genesis deadlines, or starting a new business. Doing what is hard leads to an easy life, and doing what is easy leads to a hard life.

The second half of the verse mentions the "praise and honour and glory" you'll receive if your trials are endured well, at the coming of Christ. Essentially saying, "Hey, these trials are going to be really difficult for you, extremely difficult, but it'll be all worth it in the end when you are able to stand before Christ with praise, honour, and glory." The same is true for you and me. We will have difficult times in our lives, I promise, but depending on how we handle trials, they could be to our advantage and benefit in the long run. At the end of the day, what Dave Ramsey says is true: "Live like no one else, so later you can live like no one else." He is referring to finances, but this applies to everything in life. If you choose to make sacrifices to do what is hard, you will "live like no one else." It will be a joy to look back at your life and see all that you've accomplished because you never quit.

When you have a grand vision for your life and where you want to go, **the trials and challenges pale in comparison to your dreams**. In Proverbs 29:18 (KJV) it says, "Where there is no vision, the people perish." The same is true in your life. Do you have a vision? Do you know where you are going? You can have the greatest ship in the world, but if you don't know where you are going, you will just sit at the dock your entire life.

## FAILURE IS NOT A SINGLE EVENT; IT IS A PROCESS

I once attended a sales training in Austin, Texas presented by Jeff Shore. We were required to role-play and learn new principles of selling. Before we started, Jeff encouraged us to fail. He explained that too many people are so afraid of failure that they don't try and thus never learn anything new. Instead, he promised that, if we failed, we should shout for joy, "Yes! I messed up!" He encouraged us to embrace failure because, without it, there is no learning. I have worked hard to take this to heart: When I make a mistake, I remind myself to get excited. I know that every time I fail, I get closer to getting it right! (I frequently forget and instead get discouraged, but I'm getting better.)

Set a failure quota to see how many times you can fail at something. According to John C. Maxwell, "The difference between average people and achieving people is their perception of and response to failure." The stats prove this, and studies at Tulane University by Professor Lisa Amos show that the average entrepreneur fails 3.8 times before they finally make it in business. No one starts off successful. Everyone starts at "zero followers" and moves up from there. The only thing that can keep you from succeeding is not trying at all.

When I was nineteen, I lived in Mexico for two years and learned Spanish while there. I was surrounded by other young people like myself also learning Spanish. I quickly noticed that those who were afraid to fail when they spoke never learned Spanish while those who embraced failure learned quickly and were more proficient. I made the decision to fail as many times as possible throughout a day. I would always look for opportunities to speak and fail! Then, after I failed, I would ask for help, like "How do you say that?" I would write down the words or phrases I struggled with in a notebook that I carried with me and would repeat them throughout the day.

Progress was slow. It took me over a year to roll my *r*s. In Spanish, it is crucial to do this to say the correct words. I was unable to say *perro*, which means "dog," because it requires rolling the *r*. Instead, it sounded like *pedo*, which means "fart."

Another mistake I made was, instead of telling an elderly woman that she was very nice, I told her she was sexy. You only have to do that once before you learn the difference between *ser* and *estar*. I'll share one more embarrassing moment while I sought failure learning Spanish: I was in Mexico sharing the Gospel of Jesus Christ, and I created a list of ten tips to better understand the scriptures and printed it off at the local paper store. While sharing the list with a family later that night, we arrived at number 8 on the list, which read, "Have patience." The command form of *to have*, in Spanish is *tenga*. So, it should have read "Tenga Paciencia." In Spanish, the vowel "e" is pronounced like the "a" in most English words. I spelled it Tanga, instead of Tenga. (I know that's hard to follow.) When the family's ten-year-old son read this "tip," he immediately started laughing hysterically. Apparently *tanga* means "thong." Again, I only had to make that mistake once.

I wouldn't change anything about those experiences. The failures taught me so much more than the moments of success. After one year of consistent practice, I felt 95% confident with any situation and conversation in Spanish. I was never the best, but I was never afraid to fail. In essence, don't be afraid to call an elderly woman sexy or call a dog a fart.

Strive to view failure as a steppingstone on the path to success, not a giant wall blocking the way. In all honesty, you never really fail; you just learn things that don't work. Successful people don't see failure. They see education. They see failure as a learning experienced that didn't work, ultimately moving them closer to what will work. Unsuccessful people see failure, and they are devastated and paralyzed by it.

## FAILURE IS A COMPASS

It is naive to think you can sit down and plan out every detail and aspect of their life expecting it to go exactly as planned. (You should still have a plan; just expect roadblocks.) Things will change and plans always need revision. Sometimes it's as easy as taking a different path that leads to the same outcome. Other times it's as if you were headed south one second and north the next. It's vitally important to embrace the changes that continually occur. People who cannot embrace change are like those who opposed the Model T Ford because they thought humans were destined to always ride in horse-drawn buggies. Denying change can leave you crippled, especially if you are leading a family, team, or company.

During college, Dwayne "the Rock" Johnson learned that life doesn't always go as planned. He had always planned for and dreamed of playing in the NFL, and he was well on his way. That was until he injured himself in college and subsequently missed the NFL draft. Despite this setback, he fought hard and started playing in the CFL (Canadian Football League) for a mere CA$250 per week. Just a short while later he was cut from the CFL. His dreams were shattered. He told himself this wasn't how it was supposed to happen—he was supposed to play in the NFL! That was his dream, that is what he had worked so hard to achieve! As he drove back home to Miami, he only had $7 in his wallet, which would later be the inspiration for his business, 7 Bucks Media. Years later, once the Rock could look in the rearview mirror and see where he'd come, he said, "You realize that playing in the NFL is the best thing that never happened, because it got me here . . . You have to have faith that the one thing you wanted to happen, oftentimes is the best thing that never happened."

Oftentimes, when you don't accomplish a goal, it feels like defeat. It feels like you wasted your time. But sometimes, life is pointing you in a different direction. The old saying "when one door closes another door opens" is always true! Sometimes life has a weird way of guiding us in the direction we need to go. Defeat in one area of life can fuel the fire for the next stage of life. After leaving the CFL, Dwayne decided to go into the wrestling business like several members of his family had done, including his dad. If he had never made the switch, he wouldn't be where he is today. We wouldn't have the

"Rock." Just recently, Dwayne bought the XFL (eXtreme Football League) to help people accomplish their football dreams, bringing his story full circle. Dwayne could have lived the rest of his life thinking that he was a failure for not accomplishing his goal to play in the NFL. Failure wasn't the end for the Rock; it was the beginning. I beg you to change the way you look at failure. Learn to love and embrace perceived failures.

## GROWTH VS. FIXED MINDSET

It is vital to understand the difference between a growth and fixed mindset. It is also important to understand that a person with a fixed mindset can learn to have a growth mindset and vice versa. Pay close attention to which mindset you currently possess and where you may need to make immediate adjustments.

Those with fixed mindsets believe they already have all the abilities and talents they will ever acquire in their lives. They've reached their "potential," and they've plateaued. They avoid anything that pushes them out of their current capabilities. They don't understand the concept of growth or new experiences. Those with fixed mindsets find it absurd to put themselves in a position where they might fail. The true failure for these individuals is that they have stopped growing and progressing.

Those with growth mindsets are the exact opposite. They embrace and thrive on challenges and opportunities to learn something new. The key word is *learning*. They don't see failure; they only see learning. Anything is possible if given enough time. A growth mindset individual knows, as Carol Dweck said in her book *Mindset*, "It's not always the people who start out smartest who end up the smartest." It is the work, effort, and persistence that takes you to the next level. Just like the muscle that only tears and grows under intense pressure, your skills and abilities will never improve unless you put them to the test.

Because you are reading this book and you made it to the last chapter, you likely have a growth mindset. That's great news, but growth-mindset individuals need to avoid succumbing to the pressures and influences of the fixed minded. This can happen when you share your big goals and dreams with friends and family members; they may mock you, telling you your dreams will never happen. Your mindset will become more like the mindsets of those you spend time with. When you run toward growth, expect criticism from those who have given up on their dreams.

Let me share an example of the fixed vs. growth mindset. When I was a director of sales and marketing, I encouraged fellow employees to read *The Compound Effect* by Darren Hardy. It is one of the best books to help improve your life through small actions. After reading the book, I asked everyone to submit a survey about their experience. I was ecstatic to see the progress so many had made since reading the book. They embraced a growth mindset and tried new things during the reading, pushing their limits. On the other hand, I was shocked to see that a few people actually hated the book. I couldn't believe it! One person actually said they aren't really into self-development. WHAT!? What are they into if they aren't into becoming better? One of the biggest mistakes I've made in my life is assuming that everyone around me thinks the same way I do. It's okay that not everyone thinks like you. Just don't be surprised when you tell small-minded people your big dreams and they shut them down. Don't expect everyone to believe in your goals and dreams like you do. No one will ever believe in you more than you do.

## FEAR

There are two types of fear: innate and identity. Innate fears are instinctual and save you from danger. These help you stay alive and are inherently good. If your ancestors hadn't feared saber-tooth tigers, you might not be here. If you ever come face-to-face with a lion, innate fear will kick in and notify you of danger. The same goes for spiders, snakes, and heights. Although they are innate, you can overcome these fears. That's why people can skydive and tolerate spiders crawling all over them. Innate fears likely won't make a significant difference on your success in life.

Identity fears, on the other hand, stem from the fear of shame. This is what keeps you from raising your hand to answer a question or make a comment in class. It is also what keeps you from sharing your goals and dreams with others: You're afraid of what they may or may not say. It is what keeps you from starting a business and chasing your dreams. Identity fears keep you from reaching your full potential.

At first, identity fears actually kept you safe. During the early human history, if you did something that offended the rest of the tribe, you could be banished. Banishment from the cave would lead to death, so your ancestors quickly learned to be cautious about what they did or didn't do to avoid shunning. You continue to live with these fears, but they don't have the same consequences as they once did. Although it might feel like it, you will not die from public speaking, nor is anyone going to banish you. You might feel embarrassed and your ego may take a hit, but that's as bad as it gets.

Despite lack of physical harm that comes with identity fears, millions of people let these fears kill their dreams every single day. Fear will keep you from starting because you won't feel prepared. Truthfully, you will never be fully prepared for every opportunity in life. Fortunately, there is a cure if you're willing to take the medicine: ACTION!

## ACTION > FEAR

Action cures fear. The faster the action, the faster fear is squelched. Fear is an illusion, but when you feed it with time, it grows until you become paralyzed. Analysis paralysis has kept millions of people from acting.

If you've ever cliff jumped, you know exactly what I'm talking about. Imagine you are standing at the top of a thirty-foot ledge, and you slowly creep toward the edge, peeking your head over to see what seems like a thousand-foot drop down to a deep blue death. Surviving the jump seems impossible and downright foolish. Who would put themselves in that kind of situation? The longer you peer over the edge in petrified fear, the more fear will fill your body, leaving you terror stricken. My wife experienced it while in Lake Powell. She wanted to jump off a cliff, but once she was on the edge, the fear sank in. She waited and waited, and soon her body wouldn't let her jump. She was paralyzed. She finally jumped after several failed attempts and realized it wasn't nearly as scary as her mind had built it up to be.

The reality is that we build fear in our minds to the size of the Empire State Building when, in reality, it's like the size of a grain of sand. The quick and easy fix is to take time out of the equation and take immediate action! I've found the best way to cliff jump is to jump as soon as you walk to the ledge. It's scary, but not paralyzing. The more time I give myself to think it through, the more fear my mind will create and the less likely I am to act. The same goes for starting a business, asking a cute girl to prom, asking for a raise, signing up for a triathlon, etc. When you first feel fear, act. **Feel the fear, then act.** The moment you dismiss fear, you will quickly realize how much the fear was exaggerated in your mind. Action is the antidote to curing all fear.

Analysis paralysis is especially true for salespeople. I've spoken to veteran sales reps, and the same is always true: the first cold call of the day is always scary. Because it's scary, the average sales reps avoid making the first call. If you want a list of the best excuses in the world, just ask an average sales rep. They will have millions of high-quality excuses for why right now is not a good time. They will say things like, "I can't call right now. It's too early in the morning. They aren't ready to talk to me," or, "It's almost lunch time, they are probably getting ready to leave the office," finally topping it off with, "I can't call right now. They just got back from lunch and need time for it to digest." I've heard those excuses so many times.

The best sales reps start prospecting first thing in the morning and find reasons to make right now a great time! I've found that early morning calling is ideal because successful people, who have money to buy your product, are awake early in the morning. I've made sales at all hours of the day. There is no such thing as a bad time to make a sale. Right now is the best time to act on what you fear the most!

## FEAR LEADS THE WAY

Fear often presents itself during times of uncertainty, attention, change, and struggle. Fear is present in dangerous moments, but also during moments of potential growth and learning. Avoiding uncertainty, attention, change, and struggle is good if you are actually in danger. The problem is that, most of the time, the danger isn't real, so fear robs you of growth.

Use fear as a compass to guide you. Don't be fearless. That would require an amygdalotomy, which isn't a good idea. Embrace fear. Fear is a natural human instinct. You have permission to feel fear! With time, you will realize that you'll love facing fears head-on.

Too many people get stuck letting fear run their lives. They think everyone and everything in the world is out to get them, and nothing is safe. This is not only a sad way to live, but it is also very untrue. Too many people don't follow their dreams because of the fear of failure. So what if you fail? So what? So what if people see you fail? There are over seven billion people in this world, and there is no way all of them are going to see your failure. Even if they did, it would be very low on their list of worries and concerns. You've only got one life to live, make it count.

When you face fear, you have thousands of potential outcomes racing through your mind. Pick the worst possible outcome and then ask yourself, "Is that really so bad?" As Steve Jobs said, "Remembering that you are going to die is the best way I know to avoid the trap of thinking you have something to lose. You are already naked. There is no reason not to follow your heart."

Without the sting of failure, there is no joy in success. You can't have one without the other. Where there is no struggle, there is no satisfaction. When I unicycled professionally, it was the tricks that I spent the most time failing at that felt the best when I finally landed them! Whenever a trick came easily, there wasn't as much satisfaction. On the other side of pain is pleasure.

Ralph Waldo Emerson once said, "Do the thing you fear, and the death of fear is certain." If you don't feel fear, you are too comfortable. If you are comfortable all the time, that means you aren't pushing yourself to the next level. You *should* feel fear! Fear means you are moving in the right direction!

Les Brown wisely said, "You can either live your dreams or you can live your fears." Which will you pick?

## INNOVATE OR DIE

Jeff Bezos has made billions of dollars' worth of mistakes. He says they don't "risk the farm," but they consistently try new things. In an interview with Time magazine, the Amazon CEO revealed that he gave himself a 30% chance that Amazon would succeed when he first started the company. "That's actually a very liberating expectation, expecting to fail," Bezos said. Failure and invention are inseparable twins. You *cannot* and *will not* have one without the other.

People and companies who choose not to innovate are eventually forced to do so by the marketplace. Forced innovation typically leads to bankruptcy — think Netflix's overtake of Blockbuster in Chapter 5. Bezos's words were prophetic when he told Blodget at Business Insider's 2014 Ignition conference, "What really matters is, companies that don't continue to experiment, companies that don't embrace failure, they eventually get in a desperate position where the only thing they can do is a Hail Mary bet at the very end of their corporate existence. Whereas companies that are making bets all along, even big bets, but not bet-the-company bets, prevail."

What are some things you can try today that aren't "bet-the-company" bets but could potentially be the next big thing for you or your organization?

## NEVER GIVE UP

I read a quote recently that said, "Experts fail more times than beginners even try in the first place." Most people fail because they don't try again after the first failure. Experts not only try again, they try again as quickly as possible to see what went wrong.

I'm going to myth bust something for you, and I want you to spread the word. Are you ready? THERE IS NO SUCH THING AS AN OVERNIGHT SUCCESS! The media wants you to think that it's easy because that sort of headline gets your attention, and they sell your attention. The truth is that, behind every so-called overnight success, there are thousands of hours of hard work, sweat, and consistency. Don't be fooled. If it's hard for you right now, know you are on the right path. It was hard for the person who went before you.

Refusing to give up is what makes the story and success so sweet. Always remember, if it were easy, everyone would do it. If sales were easy, every salesperson would be making minimum wage, and it would be the same as flipping burgers at McDonald's. The reason it's hard is because the reward is exceptional. Remember, a journey of a thousand miles starts with one step forward.

The true secret to success is consistency. If you only take away one thing from this book, I hope it is to be consistent. Everyone wants a six-pack, but only those who go to the gym and eat fewer calories than they burn for a sustained period of time will get that result. I'm sure you can name five people off the top of your head who said they were going to do something, did it for about a week, then gave up. Do you want to separate yourself from the pack and become outrageously successful in whatever you choose? BE CONSISTENT! The best indicator of success is obsession. I am religious about going to the gym. No matter where I am in the world, working out is something I must do every day. It's a standard I've set for myself. When I'm on vacation, I'll do crazy things to find a gym or get a workout in. Most people tell me that I'm addicted to working out or, even better, that I'm a vain person. Those things might be true, but what's the alternative? Going with the flow? Being mediocre? Allowing my environment to choose who I become? Whatever the alternative is, I don't want it. When people start calling you "obsessed" and "addicted," you are on the right path, the path of consistency.

## SUCCESS REQUIRES RISK

I recently talked with one of my cousins who quit his job of over ten years to start his own company. He said that the job was always just a steppingstone, but somehow he got trapped, paralyzed by the fear of taking a risk. He was only supposed to be at the job for a short time, but then, over ten years passed by. He was confused about why he was so scared to take the risk and start his own business. He told us that, logically, the fear didn't make sense. What's the worst thing that could happen? He fails and has to find another job? I could feel the pain of regret in his voice. He regretted not leaving sooner and wondered why he was so scared of the risk.

Taking risks is scary. It's important to understand that **success requires risk**. No risk, no reward. Think about it: To find a spouse, you risk going on dates. No dates, no marriage (unless you believe in arranged marriages). You can't fall in love without breaking your heart. To make a sale, you must contact a prospect in some way or form. All of the greatest experiences in life require risk.

The word *risk* inherently implies that there are unknowns, and the unknown are scary. Don't let that stop you. You will never have all the answers, but I promise that the universe will move in your favor to the degree you take risks.

Not all risks must be scary. I'm actually a baby when it comes to taking risks, but there is a way to make a seemingly insane risk seem like a walk in the park. I'll teach you how: When I was a professional unicyclist, I became extremely consistent at landing really hard tricks. I took risks every time I attempted a trick, but I seemed to land them nearly every time. I call it a risk, but you might call jumping down a set of ten stairs on a unicycle extremely stupid. I know a lot of unicyclists who were severely injured, breaking limbs. In my twelve-year career, I only broke a pinky finger, and it was sort of a fluke accident. It wasn't like I didn't do the crazy tricks. I was ranked 2nd in North America and 4th in the world in street riding, which required some big stunts. I'll share my secret with you. Are you ready? Okay, here it is: I started small and worked my way up to the big tricks. That's it.

Let's take, for example, the time I grinded a nearly twenty-five-foot rail. (That's a long time to balance on a unicycle.) I didn't go out one morning and say, "I've never grinded a rail on a unicycle, but let's try this twenty-five-footer on for size." That's how you get hurt. I found a small three-foot rail with grassy landings on both sides. Then I hyped myself up and tried it. I almost always failed on the first attempt. Then I got back up and tried again, making the necessary tweaks based on my first attempt. My second attempt would also likely end in failure. I'd make tweaks and try again. This could go on for a few hours or even days, but eventually I would land it. The mistake most unicyclists make is landing it once and then leaving. I would immediately land it again and again until it was second nature. Then I'd go find a four- or five-foot rail and do the same thing all over again. When you've done something a thousand times, it doesn't really seem risky anymore; it becomes second nature. So, when I tried the twenty-five-foot rail for the first time, I knew I'd done smaller railes thousands of times; this was just a little bit longer. I had confidence that I would succeed given enough time to try.

The same applies to everything in life. Start small. Try and fail at something small. Once you get it, repeat it until it becomes second nature, then try something a little bigger. Pretty soon you'll be doing things that others find outrageous, but to you, it's just another walk in the park.

Notice I never said you won't fail; I just said to start small and fail small, practice until you become a master, and then step up to a new struggle and continue to fail.

This cycle is part of your journey and is what will bring you sorrow and joy in life. Enjoy the journey; it only happens once. Sara Blakely, the owner of Spanx, once said that, every day at the dinner table, her parents would ask her what she failed at that day. Her parents taught her that it's not only okay to fail, but you should do it every day. At the end of each day, take a page out of Sara Blakley's metaphorical book and ask yourself: "What did I fail at today?"

## ENJOY YOUR JOURNEY

The journey is a gift. One of the mistakes I made was thinking, "I'll be happy when . . ." It's an easy trap to fall into, especially at a young age. I said I'd be happy when I graduated college, married the woman of my dreams, had a million dollars, drove a really nice car, etc. My happiness was always based on some event in the future. It became very unhealthy because I would see others my age who had what I wanted, and I resented them. One of my best friends was crushing it in his career, and I was envious to the point of resentment. It's a horrible, sad, and depressing way to live. It honestly doesn't make logical sense, because if your happiness is always based on something in the future, you will never be happy. There will always be something new to chase.

Let's say for example you will only be happy once you become a millionaire. What happens once you reach that goal? Does a fairy sprinkle happy dust on you, change everything, and happiness fills your body? NO! You'll never be magically happy, I promise. The human tendency is to always seek more, so inevitably, your arrival will be short-lived. Immediately after arriving at your destination or achieving your goal, you will already have another future destination planned before you have time to soak in your recent accomplishments. Can you see where this is going? No one is ever happy living this way. You will go from destination to destination, and happiness would elude you. The key is *enjoying* your journey. The "*your*" part is very important. Your journey is different than anyone else's. Comparing yourself with others robs you of happiness. ENJOY **YOUR** JOURNEY! Theodore Roosevelt said it best: "Comparison is the thief of joy."

I had an "Aha!" moment about enjoying the journey after reading *Shoe Dog* by Phil Knight, the late founder of Nike. His story is phenomenal with all the ups and downs you'd expect on the path to creating one of the most iconic brands in the world. In the last few pages of his book, he shares his secret regret. At the time he is sharing this, Phil Knight is a billionaire. He has everything money can buy. He has made it, and his company is a success. It is not presumptuous to assume that was the goal all along, right? To build a billion-dollar company is any high achiever's dream? What is Phil's secret regret? Doesn't he have it all? Well, there are actually two regrets he mentions. The first is he regrets not spending more time with his son. The second, in Phil's words, is the following: "My secret regret—that I can't do it all over again . . . how I wish I could relive the whole thing."

Every time I listen to the audiobook, my eyes fill with tears at this part of the story. In a heartfelt cry, Phil's deepest regrets are not spending more time with his son and that he can't go back and relive the experience of building Nike again. If you've read *Shoe Dog*, you'll know that his journey was no walk in the park, from being sued by a large Japanese corporation, to always being tight on cash, and everything in between. Why would he want to do all that crap again? Why not just do the good parts over again? It's because the struggle makes the joy of achievement possible. It wasn't the money, fame, or success at the end of the tunnel that made it all worth it for Phil. **It was his journey.** It was the ups and downs that brought joy and excitement. Life would be boring if it was just success. Is there really any success without failure? Or is it the failures that make success possible?

Don't spend today wishing for tomorrow to come. Spend today enjoying your journey. Spend time with the people you love. Don't sacrifice any worldly success for a failure in your relationships. If you are in the valleys of your journey, enjoy it. If you are on the mountaintops of your journey, enjoy it. CHOOSE TO ENJOY YOUR JOURNEY TODAY! Don't wait, because I know you will have the same secret regret Phil had—that you can't do it all over again.

Need motivation and more help? Scan the QR code to access free resources including my favorite motivational videos.

**CHAPTER NINE - NEVER GIVE UP**

# TAKE ACTION
## NOTHING CHANGES UNLESS SOMETHING CHANGES

- Shout "YES!" after each failure
- Follow the mantra: "The only reason I won't succeed is if I give in to failure, and I will never give in to failure."
- Spend ten minutes writing down all the things you are scared of doing. **Now pick one and start right now!**
- Ask yourself each day, **"What did I fail at today?"**
- Decide today that you will **enjoy your journey.** The good, the bad, the ugly, and the extreme success.

# FREE
# ADDITIONAL
# RESOURCES

SCAN ME

or visit TheFightAgainstMediocrity.com/Resources to download an editable PDF of the action items.

# EPILOGUE

You did it! Welcome to The Fight Against Mediocrity! We covered a lot, and I hope you received inspiration and *acted*!

The only way to change your life and the world is by acting. Talk Is Cheap, action is loud! Don't tell, show. Don't just talk the talk, walk the dang walk. Don't just dream, *do*! Everyone says they want success (however they define it), but very few are willing to do the work day in and day out. If you don't feel like it, do it anyway. The only way to escape mediocrity is daily, consistent, relentless, obsessive *action*!

The Fight Against Mediocrity is real, and you are either fighting or retreating. If you accept how things are, don't be surprised when you don't get what you want. The world will try to seduce you into "being okay with being okay." They will say things like, "Whatever happens, happens," or, "It is what it is." Don't fall for that trap. You have more potential than the universe has stars. I believe in you, and I'm rooting for your success. Choose to fight. Be sick and tired of being sick and tired. Decide today that you won't settle, because everything that settles ends up at the bottom.

As you turn this last page, I have two pieces of advice: The first is to go back to the first page and read it all over again. The brain loves repetition. You will gain new insights and cement what you learn into who you are. The second is to write down all the ideas and inspiration you've received while reading, write them down on paper, then pick the top idea that will have the biggest impact on your life and do something today. When you're done, pick another one.

I strongly urge you to complete the action items at the end of each chapter. You can find all of them at www.TheFightAgainstMediocrity.com/Resources. Imagine reading a book about gardening and then waiting near the dirt for plants to grow. Seems silly, right? When you complete the action items, you are planting the seeds of success so they can grow and flourish. Don't make the mistake of placing this book back on the shelf to collect dust. Action is the only way to change your life.

If you enjoyed this book, please share it with a friend or family member. It could be the catalyst to change their lives.

I'll see you on the battlefield.

# MORE WAYS TO FIGHT MEDIOCRITY

Have you ever felt you are capable of bigger and better things? Do you feel like you are wasting your potential? Do you want a life of freedom and impact? Scan the QR code to learn more.

TheFightAgainstMediocrity.com

Are you frustrated because you never seem to have time for yourself? You know you need to invest time into your growth, but just can't seem to make it happen. Scan the QR code for help.

TheFightAgainstMediocrity.com/Morning

# MORE WAYS TO FIGHT MEDIOCRITY

Listen to my **podcast** for FREE and learn from industry experts in sales, business, real estate, and self-development.

TheFightAgainstMediocrity.com/Podcast

Watch and subscribe to my **YouTube** channel for FREE content to help you grow your business, make more money, and Fight Mediocrity!

TheFightAgainstMediocrity.com/YouTube

# MORE WAYS TO FIGHT MEDIOCRITY

I create and share FREE content on the following platforms:

TheFightAgainstMediocrity.com/FaceBook

TheFightAgainstMediocrity.com/Instagram

# MORE WAYS TO FIGHT MEDIOCRITY

I create and share FREE content on the following platforms:

TheFightAgainstMediocrity.com/LinkedIn

TheFightAgainstMediocrity.com/TikTok

# NOTES

## CHAPTER 0

- Holland, Kimberly. "Obesity Facts in America." Healthline, Healthline Media, 29 July 2020, https://www.healthline.com/health/obesity-facts.
- Huddleston, Cameron. "Survey: 69% of Americans Have Less Than $1,000 in Savings." Yahoo!, Yahoo!, 16 Dec. 2019, https://tinyurl.com/5xtxfv8s.
- "Why 85% of People Hate Their Jobs." Staff Squared, 3 Dec. 2019, https://www.staffsquared.com/blog/why-85-of-people-hate-their-jobs/.

## CHAPTER 1

- Elder Neal A. Maxwell. "Becoming a Disciple." The Church of Jesus Christ of Latter-Day Saints, June 1996, https://www.churchofjesuschrist.org/study/ensign/1996/06/becoming-a-disciple?lang=eng.

- "3 Tips to Take Charge of Your Emotions." Tonyrobbins.com, https://www.tonyrobbins.com/mind-meaning/who-is-in-charge-of-your-emotions/.

# CHAPTER 2

- Banschick , Mark. "The High Failure Rate of Second and Third Marriages." Psychology Today, Sussex Publishers, 6 Feb. 2012, https://www.psychologytoday.com/us/blog/the-intelligent-divorce/201202/the-high-failure-rate-second-and-third-marriages.
- Hardy, Darren. Living Your Best Year Ever. 2nd ed., Reared Press, 2019.
- Press, The Associated. "Bannister, 85, Reflects 60 Years After Breaking the Four-Minute Mile (Published 2014)." The New York Times, The New York Times, 3 May 2014, https://www.nytimes.com/2014/05/04/sports/bannister-85-reflects-60-years-after-breaking-the-four-minute-mile.html.

# CHAPTER 3

- Miller, Larry H., and Doug Robinson. Driven: An Autobiography. Deseret Book, 2010.

# CHAPTER 4

- Bowker, Julie C., et al. "How BIS/BAS and Psycho-Behavioral Variables Distinguish between Social Withdrawal Subtypes during Emerging Adulthood." Personality and Individual Differences, Pergamon, 16 Aug. 2017, https://www.sciencedirect.com/science/article/abs/pii/S0191886917304920?via percent3Dihub.

- Hardy, Darren. The Compound Effect: Jumpstart Your Income, Your Life, Your Success. Hachette Go, an Imprint of Harchette Books, 2020.

- DePaulo , Bella. "Solitude, Part 2: The Benefits It Brings, and the Special Strengths of the People Who Enjoy It." Psychology Today, Sussex Publishers, 24 Mar. 2011, https://www.psychologytoday.com/blog/living-single/201103/solitude-part-2-the-benefits-it-brings-and-the-special-strengths-the.

- Warren, Katie. "11 Mind-Blowing Facts That Show Just How Wealthy Bill Gates Really Is." Business Insider, Business Insider, 4 May 2021, https://www.businessinsider.com/how-rich-is-bill-gates-net-worth-mind-blowing-facts-2019-5#2-based-on-how-much-wealthier-gates-got-in-the-past-year-he-makes-approximately-1300-per-second-according-to-business-insider-calculations-3.

- Kaufman, Scott Barry, and Carolyn Gregoire. "Executives, Protect Your Alone Time." Harvard Business Review, 16 Dec. 2015, https://hbr.org/2015/12/executives-protect-your-alone-time.

# CHAPTER 5

- Kohn, Art. "Brain Science: The Forgetting Curve–the Dirty Secret of Corporate Training." Learning Solutions Magazine, 13 Mar. 2014, https://learningsolutionsmag.com/articles/1379/brain-science-the-forgetting-curvethe-dirty-secret-of-corporate-training.
- Kohn, Art. "Brain Science: Overcoming the Forgetting Curve." Learning Solutions Magazine, 10 Apr. 2014, https://learningsolutionsmag.com/articles/1400/brain-science-overcoming-the-forgetting-curve.
- Corley, Thomas C. "How Many Books Does the Average Self-Made Millionaire Read?" Rich Habits Institute, 22 June 2015, https://richhabits.info/archives/5473.
- "People Who Read Business Books Tend to Earn More Money." Financial Post, StackCommerce, 5 Apr. 2021,

https://financialpost.com/personal-finance/business-essentials/people-who-read-business-books-tend-to-earn-more-money.

## CHAPTER 6

- Economy, Peter. "This Is the Way You Need to Write Down Your Goals for Faster Success." Inc.com, Inc., 28 Feb. 2018, https://www.inc.com/peter-economy/this-is-way-you-need-to-write-down-your-goals-for-faster-success.html.

- Rohrer, Tim. "The Value of Deadlines When Selling Radio Advertising: Sales Training Articles and Videos." Sales Gravy | Sales Training - Sales Consulting - Sales Coaching, https://salesgravy.com/human-behavior-responds-to-deadlines/.

- Stroup, Ben. "5 Reasons Why Deadlines Matter." RevOps Solutions, https://velocitystrategysolutions.com/insights/five-reasons-why-deadlines-matter.

## CHAPTER 7

- Hadfield, Ryan. "53 Sales Follow Up Statistics." ZoomInfo Blog, ZoomInfo, 1 July 2021, https://blog.zoominfo.com/sales-follow-up-statistics/.

# CHAPTER 8

- Kelli Harding, The Rabbit Effect (2019), xxiii–xxiv.

- Robert M. Nerem, Murina J. Levesque, and J. Frederick Cornhill, "Social Environment as a Factor in Diet-Induced Atherosclerosis," Science, vol. 208, no. 4451 (June 27, 1980), 1475–76.

- Stevenson, Gary E. "Hearts Knit Together." General Conference. General Conference, Apr. 2021, SLC, UT.

- Breuning , Loretta G. "The Animal Urge to Leave a Legacy." Psychology Today, Sussex Publishers, 2 Aug. 2011, https://www.psychologytoday.com/us/blog/your-neurochemical-self/201108/the-animal-urge-leave-legacy.

- Mineo, Liz. "Over Nearly 80 Years, Harvard Study Has Been Showing How to Live a Healthy and Happy Life." Harvard Gazette, Harvard Gazette, 26 Nov. 2018, https://news.harvard.edu/gazette/story/2017/04/over-nearly-80-years-harvard-study-has-been-showing-how-to-live-a-healthy-and-happy-life/.

# CHAPTER 9

- Johnson, Dwayne. "Teaching the Los Angeles Lakers How to Be World Champions." Genius Talks. 15 May 2018, Los Angeles, CA.

- Carrey, Jim. Maharishi International University of Management Graduation, 30 May 2014, Fairfield, Iowa.

- Maxwell, John C. Failing Forward: How To Make The Most Of Your Mistakes. Thomas Nelson Publishers, 2000.
- Dweck, Carol S. Mindset: The New Psychology of Success. Ballantine Books, 2016.
- Iannarino, S Anthony. "Facing the Two Types of Fears." The Sales Blog - S. Anthony Iannarino, 31 May 2019, https://www.thesalesblog.com/blog/facing-the-two-types-of-fears.

/

Made in the USA
Middletown, DE
29 March 2023

27190525R00126